The Way

Many Blessings,

The
Way

A Small Book of Wisdom

OLIVER BARDWELL

Published by Zendora Media
Post Office Box 1141
Waukee, Iowa 50325

The information in this book is designed to provide insight into spirituality, meditation and visualization. It is not meant to be used, nor should be used, to diagnose or treat any medical condition. Consult your physician before performing any of the breathing exercises contained in the book or for any medical diagnosis and treatment advice.

Cover design by May Phan
Interior book design by Jennifer Toomey
Copy editing by Nyei Murez
Author photo by Riley Shea Glenn

ISBN 978-0-578-61718-3 (paperback)
ISBN 978-0-578-62499-0 (eBook)

Printed in the United States of America

www.abookofwisdom.com

Dedication

My mother, a strong, honest, and kind woman, was my first spiritual teacher. She raised eight children in a tumultuous household with very few material resources. She once told me that during the most challenging times in her life, she could feel Christ standing right next to her, guiding her through many trials and tribulations. She said that when she was the most exhausted, worn out, and on the verge of giving up, she would pray, and be filled with such love and light that it was indescribable. My mother is a shining example of the type of love that Jesus taught. And even though she considers herself a Christian, she's never condemned and has always accepted and loved people of all faiths and backgrounds. She has taught me that truth is the same, no matter where it comes from.

I would like to dedicate this book to my mother for teaching me to seek the truth, to my children for teaching me how to love unconditionally, to my wife, for her love, compassion, and never-ending support—and to you the reader; I hope that this book will serve as a gentle reminder of who you are and what is essential in your life. May it awaken within you the desire to know your true self, that eternal and loving spirit that is beyond name and form.

To see the world in a drop of rain,
The deepest love in a ray of light,
To suffer from a stranger's pain,
And know the day in the dark of night...

Contents

Preface

THIS BOOK WAS INSPIRED AND WRITTEN AS A GUIDE TO spiritual life and a reminder of our true nature. During its writing, I awoke early almost every morning, practiced yoga, prayed, meditated, and wrote. The words flowed without difficulty or much effort, and the book seemed to write itself. I don't pretend to be an enlightened guru, sitting on a mountaintop in some faraway land; I grew up in small-town Iowa in middle America. Nevertheless, I can say with great sincerity that during the daily practice and conveyance of this wisdom, I have felt a profound and growing inner peace, and a wonderful change to my inner world.

I recently watched an interview with musician John Mayer, and when the subject of his writing came up, he said there was this place writers sometimes reach that he liked to call "the other side," and that "you don't get there very often." What he said about being in this place that I found most profound was: "While you're writing, you speak so much of your truth that even you are learning from it."

That is how I've felt in writing, reading, and editing the book you are now holding in your hands. Every time I sat down to write or edit the manuscript, I learned something.

The wisdom of *The Way* is universal and beyond the confines of any one religion. No matter what your religious beliefs, I hope you can find something within these pages that adds to and strengthens your spiritual practice.

The book is divided into three sections, each comprised of chapters on a common theme, topic, or challenge that we may face in daily life. Most chapters begin with a spiritual quote, have a short discourse on the wisdom of the topic, and are sometimes followed by poetic verses I was inspired to pen. These verses are meant to speak directly to your spirit.

I recommend reading *The Way* straight through, and then, if you're so inclined, keep it close by as a meditation guide or a tool that you can use to bring you back to your center and spirit when your mind has become immersed in a problem or challenge.

It's so easy to get caught up in the delusion of the mind and the ego that sometimes, it can help to have a small book we can pick up and turn to a page that reminds us of our true nature—a book without too much intellectual involvement, that contains words and verses that speak to our soul. I hope this small collection of wisdom can be that book for you.

Introduction

I know that *God* is not a popular word right now. Some New Age books use words like *source* or *being* instead of *God*, and that's okay. Those terms may be less off-putting for the spiritual seeker who is searching for something more. Please don't get attached to the word that is used for *God*. When you read the word *God* within this text, I welcome you to substitute it with *Divine Mother*, *Source*, *Being*, *the One Self*, or with whichever deity or term you feel most comfortable. I may even switch from one name to another at times, depending on the context. After all, God is everywhere, in all beings, in all things, and might be best described as the creative and loving force that flows through everything and all of creation.

Split a piece of wood, and I am there;
turn over a stone, and you will find me.
—GOSPEL OF THOMAS, SAYING 77

The *Tao Te Jing* says that the Tao that can be named is not the Tao. Maybe the God that can be named is not God. In the act of naming something, we separate ourselves from it. We use labels and concepts to describe a force that can only be felt, a force the mind cannot comprehend. We talk about this force's manifestations, confusing them with the force itself, or hoping they will lead us back to the experience of God.

One of my favorite movies growing up was *Enter the Dragon*. At the beginning of the film, Bruce Lee is playing an instructor who is teaching one of his students a martial arts technique. After they bow to each other, Bruce says to his student, "Kick me."

The student executes a couple of side kicks, and Bruce abruptly stops him, saying, "What was that? An exhibition? We need emotional content. Try again."

His student continues, trying once again, this time with anger. Bruce tells him anger is not emotional content. The student does the move again, this time with a different presence and strength. "That's it!" Bruce exclaims. "How did that feel?"

The student replies, "Let me think."

Just then, as a Zen master might do, Bruce smacks his student on the head, saying, "Don't think, *feel*. It's like a finger pointing a way to the moon."

The student stares at Bruce's finger as he is pointing toward the moon and receives yet another whack. There's a dramatic pause before Bruce continues, "Don't concentrate on the finger, or you will miss all the heavenly glory."

The words *God*, *Source*, *Being*, *Tao*, and *Zen* are each like a finger pointing to the moon. If we concentrate too much on the finger, we too may "miss all the heavenly glory."

God is not exclusive. We can love God or this force, by whatever name it's called and by whatever name it is worshiped. This force is love, and the act of worship is simply an expression of love. I've felt this divine presence in the fields and trees, in the small meditation room in my home, in the Christian church, in the Trappist monastery, in the Hindu ashram, and in the Buddhist temple. I've witnessed this presence in the eyes of a child, a rich man, and a beggar. We can love God wherever we find Him. In truth, He is everywhere. There is nowhere that He can't be found.

Seven Realizations

It's one thing to feel that you are on the right path, but it's another to think that yours is the only path.
—PAULO COELHO, *THE ALCHEMIST*

THERE ARE MANY PATHS TO SPIRITUAL UNDERSTANDING. No matter what religion you belong to, if you sincerely study the teachings of the spiritual master upon which your religion is based, you will find "The Way" hidden within. Sometimes in life, our spiritual practice can become confined to one trip a week or maybe only a holiday sojourn to our local church or temple. We forget that life itself is our spiritual practice, and that as we live, breathe, and interact with the world every day, we are presented with the opportunity to uncover and express our true nature. As you read this book, I'm inviting you to see how every moment of your life is part of your spiritual journey.

Following are seven realizations of "The Way," as I have found them in the sacred scriptures of the world and along my own spiritual journey. I welcome you to explore them and to adopt them into your practice, either in their entirety or in part, in whatever way feels right to you.

I
Oneness

God, Being or Source permeates the universe, and underlies and resides within all beings and all creation. Nothing exists that isn't made up of this creative and loving force.

II
Original Goodness

We are all children of this force, children of God. Living in joy, happiness, love, and prosperity is our birthright. We have the free will to choose this birthright or to turn away from it.

III
Presence

By practicing meditation, prayer, and mindfulness, we can learn to experience our connection to this loving force and bring its presence into our daily lives.

IV
Gratitude

Cultivating joy and gratitude allows us to open our hearts and experience a world of infinite possibilities.

V
Suffering

In times of trial, learning to embrace and understand our suffering and the suffering of others allows us to open our hearts further and to cultivate empathy, understanding, and forgiveness.

VI
Compassion

Expressing compassion and loving-kindness to others teaches us to share our divinity with the world.

VII
A Life of Purpose

There is no one like you in the universe. You are unique and made up of the stuff of stars. You are here to discover your dharma, develop your unique talents, and share them with the world. It's never too late.

PART I:

Inner and Outer Reality

Inner Peace

For behold, the kingdom of God is within you.

—LUKE 17:21

Your vision will become clear when you
can look into your own heart.
Who looks outside dreams, who looks inside awakes.

—CARL JUNG

THE DOORWAY TO THE KINGDOM OF HEAVEN IS WITHIN you. It is ever-present, beyond the many layers of mind and ego, beyond regrets about yesterday and worries about tomorrow.

I remember reading a Sunday school story once about some people from long ago who needed to help God hide. It was a beautiful story designed to help the children think and interact with the teacher and to help them realize how close God truly is. The people from long ago thought to hide God in the mountains but knew that when someone was walking through the mountains and witnessed their beauty, they would realize that God was there. They thought to hide Him in the Ocean but knew that when people saw the wonders of the Ocean, they would know that God was there. Should they hide Him in the grasses of the plains? Or should they hide God in the trees of the forest? Finally, they decided the best place to hide God would be in the human heart. They thought few people would look inside themselves to find God.

They were right. How often do we take the time to look inside ourselves? Most of the time, our attention is focused outward. From the minute we wake up in the morning until we close our eyes to go to sleep at night, we are bombarded with external stimuli. What we fail to realize is that there is a whole universe within us. When we open our hearts, look inside ourselves, and feel the love that's always there, we've found inner peace. We've found God.

Practice: I invite you to remember a time you felt truly at peace, with love flowing in your heart. It could have been when you were alone in nature or with a significant other, or when you were spending time with your family and completely present in the moment. Your thoughts and mental judgments may have slowed down, or temporarily ceased. Whatever experience this was for you, it is still there, and you can access it at any time. All you have to do is close your eyes and put yourself there. Take a deep breath and exhale slowly. Become aware of your body and allow your breathing to slow. Imagine what you experienced. See what you could see. Hear what you could hear. Feel what you felt. Now just focus on the joy and inner peace of that moment and feel it now. No sorrows. No worries. No pain. No suffering. Only joy and peace. As you sink into this feeling of inner peace, you may feel immersed in warm, enveloping light, love, and peace, extending endlessly, in all directions. Allow yourself to experience this state of inner peace.

After some time enjoying this peace, think of a recent experience that didn't go so well or of a future situation where you might need this extra resource. Now imagine the scene of the past or future experience playing out on the movie screen of your mind. You could be experiencing the situation from the inside, or as an observer. If you are thinking of a past situation, imagine how bringing your inner peace would have changed the outcome. If you're thinking of a potential future situation, how does it play out when you bring your inner peace to it? Once you've done the exercise, let it go. The past is gone—it's only one version of a story we like to tell ourselves; and the future doesn't exist. There is only the present. Repeating this practice can change how you feel about something that happened in the past, and better prepare you for a potential challenge that you may be concerned about in the future.

When you learn to cultivate this presence, to sit in stillness or to be in the moment, whether you're alone in nature, or in a crowded city, it will allow you and those around you to experience this peace.

The Buddha called this state of peace *nirvana*: a place of no suffering, a state beyond the cycle of death and rebirth. At a deeper level, this feeling, this place of peace is oneness with God, the Source, or the Creator; it is the vast light and cosmic song beyond our physical senses, underlying and emanating throughout eternity and the many worlds within it.

Peace love light eternal
Never-ending joy and happiness
No sorrow
No pain
No suffering
Like a sleeping child
Being held to the bosom of the Divine Mother

The child, tired of playing in the sea of desire
Ever longing and searching for God
Through vigilance and lifetimes of unceasing effort
Escapes the clutches of Mara the Tempter
Conquers the delusion of Maya
And, at long last, returns home.

Spiritual Masters

*The teachings of a spiritual master ignite the fire for
love and wisdom within us and serve as a road map to
attaining self-realization.*

CHRIST, ENOCH, MOSES, BUDDHA, KRISHNA, SHIVA,
Shakti, Patanjali, Lao Tzu, enlightened beings, illumined
saints and sages, spiritual masters, and teachers—there are
too many to name. Every age and culture have their spiritual teachers and messengers. We are taught about the ones
that our culture or society is aware of, and upon whose lives
and teachings our religions are built. But because there are
multitudes of souls—spanning thousands of years and the
far reaches of the globe—who have suffered, and are still
suffering and aching for spiritual understanding, there is a
need for many loving beings and spiritual teachers.

Much can be said about the unity of all religions: the
parallels between what Jesus taught in the Sermon on the
Mount and in the Eight-Fold Path and the Four Noble

Truths of Buddhism, the commonalities in what Krishna and Jesus both taught about loving God. It's in the common themes and teachings of all great faiths that we can find spiritual truth and begin to understand our brothers and sisters who practice the different religions of the world.

I once participated in a symposium on world peace in Denver, Colorado. I believe there were representatives from most of the major religions around the globe. They were all there discussing how the commonalities of our spiritual practices could bring us all together and help us to overcome our cultural differences. It was inspiring to witness spiritual leaders from all different backgrounds supporting each other and expressing ideas of peace and compassion—ideas that should be the theme and practice of all religions and religious leaders. We should be building bridges between ourselves and our brothers and sisters of different faiths.

When we learn to look past rituals and manmade religious dogma—which have, at times, come to hide the true spiritual teachings of the enlightened beings at the root of our religions—we begin to uncover the one spiritual teacher whose light and wisdom shines through it all.

Practice: Find a spiritual being or a teacher whose message resonates with you. If you have a religion that you currently practice and already feel an affinity with its messiah or prophet, try to develop a personal relationship with them. I mentioned in the dedication that there were times in my mother's life when she felt Christ standing right beside her, sending her strength, peace, and love. I've felt this too, and you can feel it as well. Once, when I was preparing for a difficult mediation, I prayed to Christ to be with me, to protect me and help guide me through the trials of the day. I prayed that he would help everyone involved to come to a resolution, and he did. He was there next to me. I felt his presence and peace in every moment. The mediation lasted over eight hours, and the opposing attorney had no intention of coming to an agreement. My counsel couldn't believe how calm and unmoved I was throughout the proceedings. Even the mediator was amazed. By the end of the day, my counsel was exhausted, and our mediator was exasperated with the other attorney. I never once felt tired or upset. Even while under attack, I was able to remain calm and centered. My friend and brother Christ was there with me, with his hand on my shoulder. I knew that it would work out. Much to everyone's surprise, both sides came to an amicable agreement and entered into a temporary order that was beneficial to everyone involved. When we finally left for the day, I felt refreshed and at peace.

Think of your spiritual teacher as your loving father or mother, or as your older brother or sister—as someone who can guide you along your spiritual journey, whose love and knowledge can help light your way. Study their teachings. Make them a part of your everyday life. Talk to them in prayer, commune with them in meditation, and know that they are always available to you.

When the world cries out
A master comes
One who has conquered themselves and destroyed the ego
One free from desires
One who has seen through the illusion
Who has transcended this world and the worlds beyond
Who has escaped the cycle of death and rebirth

They fully reside in the Kingdom of Heaven
Emanating love, light, peace, and compassion
Their message is one of love and hope
They are an example of who we are meant to be

Seek one of these lights
Let their teachings shine upon you
Illuminating the way through the darkness
To the wellspring of all light

In the family of God
When one brother or sister
Finds the way back to our mother and father
They will always return to show us the way

And when the world pulls you from the path
When there seems to be only darkness
Take shelter in the love and teachings
Of those who have gone before.

Who We Are

*I have said Ye are gods, and that all of
you are children of the most high.*

—PSALMS 82:6

The Buddha is in you.

—THICH NHAT HANH

Is it not written in your law, "I said, Ye are gods"?

—JOHN 10:34

WHO DO YOU SAY YOU ARE WHEN YOU INTRODUCE YOUR-
self upon first meeting someone, or when you're at a lunch
group, and everyone is going around the table giving intro-
ductions? It's your turn, and you say, "My name is so-and-
so, and I am a such-and-such." It may sound something like,
"My name is Jan (or John), and I'm an investment banker.
I have a master's degree from Iowa State University. I am
married and have two children: Johnny Jr. and Ava."

I've struggled with that question at times. My wife and I sometimes joke about how I need five different business cards depending on the situation and on a person's need. I had someone recently ask me to come to her networking group. I wondered what I would tell the group when it was my turn to introduce myself. "Hi, my name is Oliver Bardwell. It's a pleasure to be here. Thanks for inviting me. I own a residential and commercial interiors company. I am a home builder and developer. I'm an author, life coach, business consultant, and real estate investor. I'm a husband, a son, a brother, a friend. I'm a soccer coach, a martial artist and a photographer. My most important role has been being a dad. I meditate and practice yoga and try to see every moment as part of our spiritual journey. I am a divine being, as you all are, sharing this human experience with you. How can I help you on your journey?" That last part might be interesting.

We define ourselves with names and forms, or sometimes, with what we've accomplished and how much money we have in our various investments and our 401K. Maybe it's by the type of car we drive, the clothes we wear, our favorite hobby, or the number of followers we have on our social media accounts.

We are actually none of these things. These are things with which we identify. That identification is part of the ego, the make-believe façade that hides our true self.

When asked who you are, you have probably never thought or said, "I am a Divine Being, having a human experience. I am that I am."

You *are* a Being of Light, having a human experience. You have forgotten your divinity. Beyond the mind and the ego is your true self. To realize this self is the purpose of life.

Practice: Sit quietly and focus on your breath. Allow your mind to follow each inhalation and exhalation. Now imagine all the roles you play in life, all the ways that you define yourself, and the ways others may define you. Maybe it's as a mother, father, husband or wife, daughter, son, boyfriend or girlfriend or by your profession or sport; maybe it's as a student or a teacher. Imagine yourself in those roles and let each pass away, one by one, one after another, until there are none left. Now, as all the roles have faded, relax into what's left, what's been obscured by the demands and expectations of the world, that deep inner being. As you open yourself up to who you are beyond names and forms, enjoy the peace, love, and light that fills you and flows through you.

Beings of Light
Walking in Darkness
Forgetting who they are
And from where they came   23

Beings of Light
Clouded in Darkness
Bowing their heads in sorrow
And in shame

Stop playing in the storm of desire
Begin looking inward to the light of your soul

Uncovering your light
And dispelling the darkness
Make it your life's most important goal

When your soul shines brightly
And you walk in the world
You will become a beacon of hope

A brilliant reminder of who we truly are
And of what we inherently know

You are a Divine Being
Having a human experience
Awaken to your divinity.

Karma

For whatsoever a man soweth; that shall he also reap.
—GALATIANS 6:7

Before you act, you have freedom, but after you act, the
effect of that act will follow you whether you want it to
or not. That is the law of karma.
—PARAMAHANSA YOGANANDA

The doer of evil reaps suffering
Here and Hereafter
In both states remembering, "I have committed evil."
Not only here, but hereafter, he experiences
More suffering because he has gone to a state of
suffering.

The doer of good deeds reaps happiness,
Here and Hereafter,
In both states remembering, "I have done good deeds."
And there is more joy
Because he has gone to a blissful state.

—THE DHAMMAPADA 1:16–17

KARMA IS LIKE NEWTON'S THIRD LAW OF MOTION: *Every action has an equal and opposite reaction.* It's ingrained in our very essence. Reference to this force can be found in almost every great scripture.

There are three types of karma in action: physical, verbal, and mental. Everything we do, say, and even think are like seeds planted in the ground that will someday take root. It's important to realize this and to live our daily lives with the understanding that someday, everything we sow—both good and bad—we will surely reap.

A wise spiritual teacher, J.P Vaswani, the author of *What Would You Like to Know About Karma,* said, *When we begin to understand the concept of Karma, we will never, ever blame God for anything that happens to us. We will realize that we are responsible for all that happens to us.*

When you read that, you may think, "Well, what about the innocent young man in the wheelchair? Or the child who was just diagnosed with cancer? What did they do to deserve their circumstances?" I've often pondered the same questions.

In Eastern thought, it's believed there is karma we are born into this life with, generated in other lifetimes, and karma generated in this life. There is little that we can do about the karma we were born into this life with, other than to accept it and try our best not to blame others or some outside force for our circumstances. Whatever the karma may be, whether we consider it positive or negative, it just is. We can easily recognize the karma that we are generating in this life. All we have to do is look around, and if we are honest with ourselves, we can see how every action and belief from our past, empowering or disempowering, has brought us to where we are and what we are experiencing today.

Practice: How can we accept the hand we've been dealt in life and turn our life circumstance into a steppingstone on the path of our spiritual journey? The most important questions about the things in life over which we have no control aren't, "Why did it happen? Why me? Why them? Why now?" The most important questions are: "How can I find an empowering meaning in this experience?" "How can I accept what is and move forward in a way that is in alignment with my true nature, and a benefit to myself and others?" Remember, you will always get the answers to the questions you ask yourself, so it's vital to ask quality questions.

Look at your life and your current circumstance. Think of an area of your life you aren't happy with. How can you take responsibility for the actions or inactions that have brought you to this place? List all the things you have done or failed to do that created this circumstance—whether it's a troubled relationship or a lack of one, or a challenge in your health or current financial situation. The first step in creating a positive change in any area of your life is in being able to accept and take ownership of how you arrived at where you are now.

Karma follows us throughout our lives
In this life and into the worlds beyond

An energy, positive and negative
That is generated by our actions

Everything we are experiencing now
Is a direct result of those past thoughts and actions

Even in death, we are unable to escape Karma

Our thoughts and actions have vibrations
Higher and lower
Good and evil
Positive and negative

When we shed this body
Like an old, worn-out suit of clothes
And only the astral and causal bodies remain

It is the vibration of our thoughts and our accumulated actions
That ferry us to the next realm

Those of higher thoughts, actions, and vibrations
Experience higher, lighter planes of existence
These have been called heavens
And are the states of existence in which we reap the
Rewards of good Karma

Those of lower thoughts, actions, and vibrations
Experience lower, darker planes of existence
These have been called hells
And are the states of existence in which heavy debts of
Negative Karma are balanced

Then, if we still have earthly desires and earthly Karma,
When the circumstances are right
We are born again to the right parents, family, and situation
Determined by our remaining Karmic balance.

Love

You must love in such a way that
the person you love feels free.
—THICH NHAT HANH

Love your enemies, bless them that curse you,
do good to them that hate you, and pray for them
that spitefully use you and persecute you.
—MATTHEW 5:44

Thou shalt love thy neighbor as thyself.
—MARK 12:31

WHAT IS LOVE? THERE ARE MANY TYPES OF LOVE: THE love that exists between parents and children; the love that exists between husband and wife; the love of family; the love of friends. When everyone is getting what they want out of these relationships, they seem to feel wonderful. But when those involved are not getting what they want, drama ensues. This kind of love can become selfish, with conditions and ideas like "me and mine."

There is love that draws boundaries: Love of country, love of gender, love of race, love of religion. Love like this discriminates between "us and them" and can even lead to prejudice. If someone is outside of what we consider to be our circle of love, there can be indifference or even hostility.

And how easy it can be to go from inside to outside someone's circle of love. How many times has someone said, "I love you" only to then say, "I hate you" during a breakup or divorce, and then do terrible things to you? How many times have you said or thought you loved someone only to turn around and do the same terrible things to them? This isn't true love. This is immature and ignorant love.

True love is ever-flowing and unconditional; it extends to all living beings. True love is the only emotion that emanates from God. True love is an expression of the Divine. As Jesus said so simply, *God is love*.

Someone close to me had a brief glimpse of what Zen practitioners would call *satori*. He felt peaceful, present, and blissful in doing his work and in all his daily activities. He told me that when it faded, it scared him, because in that state, he had loved everyone the same way he loved his children, and he felt that it must have made his love for his children less special.

In essence, like the great Thich Nhat Hanh, my friend had briefly expanded his circle of love to all humanity, instead of only to his immediate family. What he had failed to see was that while in the state of feeling his Oneness in Being, along with loving all humanity as if they were his own children, he loved his actual children *even more* than he had before. How beautiful a thing to glimpse in this lifetime, and how tragic a thing to become afraid of once it begins to fade. But it's a blessing to glimpse this state of our divinity, and I have faith that with practice, my friend will find it again.

Practice: Try to cultivate true and spiritual love in your relationships. One way to do this is to go to the relationship only to give without expecting anything in return. Give your time, yourself, your love and encouragement.

Start with your significant other, and then your family and those closest to you. In doing this, you will begin to see incredible changes in your relationships.

Then extend your love and kindness to friends, and to strangers, and notice the positive changes that occur.

Finally, extend your love and kindness to people that you don't like or toward whom you may be harboring resentment. Jesus said, *Love your enemies and pray for those who persecute you.* Expand your circle until your ability to love and to give has no boundaries.

You may find that the more you give, the more your capacity and desire to give will grow. Being able to do this will change your life and the lives of those around you.

God is love
Emanating throughout the universe
Love that can be found at the core of every being
Underneath the dirt and grime of the ego
Beyond the static of the mind

Love your enemies
Love your neighbor
Respond to anger with lovingkindness
Respond to ignorance with loving patience
Respond to sorrow and injury with loving compassion

Love ties the world together
Hate and anger tears it apart

The wise person is patient, loving, and kind
Don't mistake being loving with weakness
One can be loving and firm
Loving and resolute
Loving and determined

Love is God's peace
When irritation arises
Filter it through God's peace
When anger threatens
Shower it with God's peace

Any action taken in true love
Is an expression of the divinity
That resides in all beings.

Kindness

This is my simple religion: No need for temples;
no need for complicated philosophy. Your own mind,
your own heart, is the temple.
Your philosophy is simple kindness.
—DALAI LAMA

The simplest acts of kindness are, by far, more powerful
than a thousand heads bowing in prayer.
—MAHATMA GANDHI

BEING KIND, WHEN PRACTICED OFTEN, BECOMES A BEAU-
tiful habit, a way of being. Acts of kindness take such little
effort, but we can get so lost and caught up in the turmoil
of our day that we forget how powerful they can be, and
how wonderful an effect one small and kind act can have
on the lives of those around us.

My son and I recently attended a funeral for a young
high school senior who had passed away suddenly. It was

a sad and solemn affair. It's always heartbreaking when someone young leaves this life so unexpectedly. Though our families were close when this young man was in elementary school and junior high, I didn't know him well as a teenager. During the funeral service, one of his teachers went up to the podium to read something that the young man's mother had written. She listed words that described his many great qualities and told stories about each one. One of the many qualities that she talked about was kindness.

To illustrate this, the woman spoke about how the young man had a real zest for life and was very active in sports. One of his favorite sports was basketball. During a game, his mother noticed another player wearing her son's orange basketball shoes. They were her son's favorite pair from the year before. After the game, she asked her son about it, and he simply said, "He needed a pair and couldn't afford to buy them, so I gave him mine." He didn't have to mull it over or consult with anyone; he just did what he thought was right.

The young man also struggled with an autoimmune disorder called alopecia, which can cause hair loss. Once, while playing in a baseball game, he noticed a child who had also lost his hair, watching the game from the sidelines. After the game, he went over to the child, squatted down, and removed his baseball cap. He just wanted the young boy to know that he had lost his hair, too, and that the boy wasn't alone.

He was always going out of his way to help someone or to perform a random act of kindness. You could tell from the hundreds of people at his service how much of an effect this had had on the people around him and on our community. From the children in his mother's classroom where he often volunteered, to friends and family, to teachers and faculty, to classmates and teammates, and even to players on opposing teams, the effect of his kindness was palpable.

In our daily lives, we are often presented with opportunities to express the kindness that is inherent in our nature. An act of kindness can be as simple as smiling at someone, giving them a sincere compliment or offering to return their shopping cart after they've unloaded their groceries. It's always a nice feeling and pleasant surprise when you pull up to the coffee shop window, and the cashier says, "The person ahead of you paid for your order."

One Christmas, while I was picking up some last-minute gifts, the woman checking out in front of me was struggling to get her government assistance card to work. She didn't seem to speak English very well and was having difficulty understanding the cashier. He was trying to tell her that there was no credit left on the card. It was easy to see they were both becoming frustrated by the situation. I glanced at the woman's cart and saw that it was full of meat and fresh vegetables. It looked as if she had a large family to feed.

When I took out my credit card and told the cashier that I would pay for her groceries, she was beside herself with gratitude.

Every one of us can be a small beacon of hope in someone else's life. The more we do to bring joy to the lives of those around us, the more connected we feel to ourselves and to the one being that resides in us all

Practice: Begin with your spouse, or a family member, or friend. An act of kindness can be as simple as a smile or a positive comment. It can be a small act of service or a thoughtful gift. My wife has this way of smiling at me when I walk into the room that makes me feel like something special is taking place. It never fails to amaze me. Simply recognizing your child's accomplishments and talents in a positive way, if done consistently, can affect the course of their life.

As you practice kindness, don't expect anything in return. Giving with the expectation of receiving something in return is not giving; it's trading. What you gain from being kind is the knowledge that you helped make someone's day a little brighter. You may have even helped ease someone's suffering.

Don't stop with your family and friends. Extend that same kindness to everyone you meet in life: A kind smile, a word of encouragement, an act of service. Before you know it, you will become a positive ripple in the fabric of society.

Be kind
It takes little effort
Don't be afraid your kindness might be rejected
And you'll appear the fool

It's better to have peace in your heart
And kindness rejected
Than to be caught up in drama and delusion.

A master sits on a riverbank
A scorpion falls in the water

As the master rescues the scorpion
The scorpion stings him

The scorpion falls in again
The master plucks him out
And is stung once more

A little while later
Another scorpion falls in
The master reaches out to rescue it
A passing villager says
"Master, don't!
You will get stung again!"

The master replies
"It is a scorpion's dharma to sting
And it is a human being's dharma to be kind."

Forgiveness

The weak can never forgive.
Forgiveness is the attribute of the strong.
—MAHATMA GANDHI

When you produce a thought that is full of under-
standing, forgiveness, and compassion, that thought
will immediately have a healing effect on both your
physical and mental health, and on those around you. If
you think a thought that is full of judgment and anger,
that thought will immediately poison your body and
mind, and the people around you.
—THICH NHAT HANH

ONE OF THE KEYS TO FORGIVENESS IS UNDERSTANDING. You don't have to condone someone's actions to understand them, but when you understand someone you feel has wronged you, you can find compassion for them and will no longer hold onto resentment.

Forgiveness is unnecessary if you are so at peace with yourself that you are unaffected by the actions of others.

Once, there was a wealthy merchant whose children were meditating with the Buddha and his disciples every morning. The merchant believed his children were "wasting time and being led astray," so he went to confront the Buddha, becoming so angry that he actually spit on the Buddha's face. The Buddha's disciples were outraged. The Buddha just wiped his face, smiled, and said nothing. The merchant stormed off.

That night, the merchant couldn't sleep. He tossed and turned, feeling tormented and remorseful. The next day, he went to the Buddha and knelt at his feet, begging for forgiveness.

The Buddha said, "For what do you need to be forgiven?"

The merchant replied in surprise and anguish, "I'm the man who spat on you yesterday."

The Buddha just smiled and said, "I am not the same person who was sitting here yesterday. If I see him, I will be sure to tell him you are sorry."

We are all Buddhas. Why should we let the events of the past or the hallucinations of tomorrow have any effect on us?

While he was on the cross, Jesus said, "Father forgive them for they know not what they do." If Jesus could pray for the forgiveness of his persecutors while suffering on the cross, can we not forgive someone for whom we have been harboring resentment?

Try taking some time to understand those you feel may have wronged you, take into consideration their background, beliefs, and circumstances. Understanding is not condoning, but it is the first step toward forgiveness, and ridding yourself of the poison of anger and resentment.

Practice: Sit quietly in a comfortable position. Become aware of each inhalation and exhalation. As your breathing begins to slow, begin bringing relaxation to your body and mind. Starting with your feet, imagine a wave of warm, relaxing energy spreading up through your ankles, calves, knees, thighs, hips, and midsection. You may see this energy as a bright white light. This warm, white, and healing light continues to rise through your hands and arms, chest, back and shoulders, neck and head, releasing any tension you may have been holding onto. As you sink into this deep relaxation, imagine that you are going on a journey of forgiveness. Starting from when you were a child, remember a time you may have wronged someone and hurt their feelings. You may have said or done something in ignorance. Send love to that person and ask for forgiveness. Think of another time, and another time. Each time, send love and request forgiveness. Continue through your life, remembering similar instances as a young adult, and as an adult. Each time, send your love and regret and request forgiveness.

And: now that you have requested forgiveness for things you may have done to cause others pain and suffering, it's time to practice forgiving others. Remember a time as a child when someone did or said something that hurt your feelings or caused you to suffer. Send them love and forgiveness. Open your heart and let go of any resentment you have been holding onto. Travel forward to young adulthood and do the same. Take your time doing this. Think of anyone toward whom you may be harboring ill will, and imagine them before you. Surround them in bright, loving light. Send them love and forgiveness. Let your resentment go. Imagine all the negative energy you've been holding onto being released and replaced by love and light radiating from the eternal well within.

Only the ignorant drink poison
Expecting that someone else will suffer from it
Harboring hate and resentment
Is drinking poison

Forgive quickly
Don't be unsettled by the ignorance of others

Don't seek vengeance, even in your mind
Where it will fester like an untended wound
Causing you pain and distraction
Souring the rest of your life

Practice understanding and patience
Love and compassion
Knowing that your peace is your peace alone
Always there and ever-present

No one can touch it
Except those whom you choose to share it with.

Gratitude

I would maintain that thanks are the highest form of thought, and that gratitude is happiness doubled by wonder.

—G. K. CHESTERTON

The single greatest thing that you can do to change your life today would be to start being grateful for what you have right now.

—OPRAH WINFREY

ONE DAY, IN MY MID-TWENTIES, I WAS WATCHING TELE-vision, and an episode of *The Oprah Winfrey Show* came on. I don't remember who her guest was, but I do remember Oprah talking about how keeping a gratitude journal had changed her life. It truly resonated with me, so every night before going to bed, I began writing down in my journal several things that I was grateful for. The common theme I noticed, when reading back through those journals, was that I was most grateful for the people in my life. Gratitude started with my connection to God, then family, and then moved outward into the world. Health was an important theme. I was thankful for my breath and strong heart. Then, I began writing down "magic moments," things that happened throughout the day that seemed to sparkle with the miraculous. The interesting thing is that because I knew that later in the day I would be writing these things down, I started looking for them everywhere. I began *looking* for magic. *Looking* for things to be grateful for. Now, there isn't a day that goes by when I don't experience a certain amount of wonder in life.

If you have ever sat and listened to Thich Nhat Hanh speak, you may have realized he experiences wonder in every moment. His wonder is childlike. He is calm and serene, gentle and peaceful. His speech is intimate. *Look at the beautiful flower. Breathing in, I see the beautiful flower, and breathing out, I smile.*

This is the essence of the life and joy we were born to experience.

Practice: It's too easy to get caught up in this hectic, fast-paced society and find ourselves in constant pursuit of what we don't have, with too much focus on what is lacking in our lives. Learn to turn your attention to the myriad of things in your life you can be grateful for. At the end of each day, write down several things you are grateful for, and then list a few magic moments. If you do this daily, it will change your life. You will begin to live a life of thanks and gratitude.

Thank you for the Mother Earth
And for the beautiful sky above
Thank you for your cosmic song
And for filling my heart with love

Thank you for your sincere smile
On the random passerby
Thank you for the unbounded Joy
That makes me feel that I could fly

I'm grateful for your every breath
That brings the winds of peace
And thankful for this magic moment
That allows my worries to cease.

Live in gratitude
Open your heart
Find the magic in every moment.

Mindfulness

*When we are mindful, deeply in touch with the present
moment, our understanding of what is going on
deepens, and we begin to be filled with acceptance, joy,
peace, and love. Mindfulness is learning how to fall in
love with ordinary things.*

—THICH NHAT HANH

*Which of you, by taking thought, can add one cubit
to his stature?...Take, therefore, no thought for the
morrow; for the morrow shall take thought for the
things of itself.*

—MATTHEW 6:27, 6:34

THERE HAS BEEN A LOT OF TALK ABOUT "MINDFULNESS"
lately. We hear about it on TV, and in books and maga-
zines, and on the internet. There is even a trend toward
mindfulness training in the workplace.

I recently read *The Life-Changing Magic of Tidying Up* and *Spark Joy* by Marie Kondo. She has made it her life's work to help people find joy in decluttering their homes and lives. Although I don't think she ever mentions the term "mindfulness" in either book, she applies the thirteenth-century Zen master Dogen's philosophy of "intimacy in all things" to folding clothes and letting no-longer-needed possessions go. Completely present as she lovingly smooths each fold in a T-shirt, Marie thanks the shirt for its service. While reading about her philosophy on how to treat clothing and other personal items that have served you, I was reminded of St. Francis, gently talking to the birds, animals, flowers, and trees. Now, I love to fold my clothes. Folding clothes has become a beautiful meditation for me.

Mindfulness is simply being present in the moment: in *any* moment, in *every* moment, doing what you're doing without indulging in the running commentary of your mind; just *being*. With this practice comes an inner expansion, and joy that is beyond description.

Practice: Try being mindful in your daily activities. If you find your thoughts constantly wandering, bring part of your focus to your breath. If this proves to be difficult, count your exhalations, and if you happen to make it to 100, start over or just continue breathing with silent awareness. You can count your breaths while doing anything you would normally do instead of daydreaming about tomorrow or regretting the past.

There is no reality beyond this moment
The past is a dream
A story you are telling yourself and others
So why keep going there?

The future doesn't exist
It is another story of what might be
So why keep going there?

Make-believe past
Make-believe future
Mental movies
Over and over and over

Come back
Be here now
Come back
Be here now

When you're doing dishes
Do dishes

When you're sweeping the floor
Sweep the floor

When you're folding your clothes
Fold your clothes

When you are with a friend
Be with your friend

Do everything with intimacy and joy.

Dwell in reality
Dwell in the moment
Connect with the Self
Connect with the world.

Find God in this breath
Find God in that flower
Find God in that smile

The doorway to the Kingdom of Heaven
Is here and now.

Presence

pres·ence *[noun] – the state or fact of existing,*
occurring, or being present.
—*OXFORD ENGLISH DICTIONARY*

Presence is a sense of inner spaciousness.
—ECKHART TOLLE

WITH MINDFULNESS COMES PRESENCE. WHEN YOU ARE
mindful and focused on the moment at hand, you bring
your full presence to a situation.

I always talk to my children about this: *When you're in*
class at school, be in class at school. Be attentive; be present. When
you are at practice, be at practice. Give 100 percent. If you're not
present, you aren't able to do this.

It's reflected in their grades and what the teachers say
about them at conferences. It's reflected in the type of
friend they are and in the amount of happiness and confi-
dence they have in life.

One time, a family member was struggling with a life situation and wanted to meet with me to talk. We met at a coffee shop, and I could see he was very distraught. All I brought was my presence. I offered no thoughts, no judgments, and no advice. But I was completely conscious of the moment: connected, joyful, projecting love, present. Within moments, I could tell he felt better and had come up with a solution to his problem.

Another time, a friend invited me out to a restaurant to talk. He had recently gone through a divorce and had signed up for a new dating app on his phone. It was constantly going off, and he was spending a lot of time replying to messages. I finally said, "Friend, if you need alone time with your phone, I don't mind." Awakened to the present moment, he apologized, put his phone away, and we had a nice conversation over dinner.

Practice: It's easy to tell when someone is present or when their mind is elsewhere—even if their face isn't buried in a gadget. There is no moment that is not worth being present for. Instead of thinking about the next profound thing that you want to say or about where you'd rather be while you're listening to your friend or loved one, truly listen and be there. Shut the ringer off on your phone, and bring the wandering part of your mind to your breath. Listen to what the other person is saying and then listen to that which is beyond what they are saying, which lies in the silence between spoken words. Let them feel your full presence.

Be present always

Your presence is felt
It's tangible
It's important
It's Holy
It's Divine
It's a gift

Presence can fill a room
Presence can build bridges
Presence brings all your resources to bear

Every moment can be beautiful
If you show up for it

Don't miss the beautiful flower
The clear blue sky
The whisper on the breeze
The touch of your loved one's hand
The smile of a passerby
The meaning behind the words
Or the presence of God in all things.

Nonjudgment

Whosoever judges others digs a pit for themselves.

—BUDDHA

Judge not, that ye be not judged. For with what judgment ye judge, ye shall be judged: and with what measure ye mete, it shall be measured to you again.

—MATTHEW 7:1–2

Recognizing our own flaws and past mistakes allows us to accept others' shortcomings and understand where they are on their own spiritual journey.

NONJUDGMENT IS ONE OF THE CORE TEACHINGS OF ALL spiritual masters. Judgment divides us. When you judge, you are saying, "I am better than them," and "My beliefs are right; theirs are wrong."

Unfortunately, our ego thrives on judgment.

When I was young, I ran into a master—almost literally. My brother and I had driven twenty hours to stay at an ashram so that we could meet an illumined guru. We were exploring the grounds, and as we walked around the corner, there he was.

I was surprised and didn't know what to say; so, knowing he was from India, I said, "How do you like America?"

He replied simply, "It's all the same."

I don't know if he was enlightened. They had built up a beautiful temple around him, and he had many disciples. That doesn't necessarily make someone enlightened. But, the statement he made was an enlightened statement: *It's all the same.*

Nonjudgment. Dark, light, cold, hot, this or that. If you're residing in the Kingdom of Heaven, if you feel inner peace and Oneness with all things at your core, and it radiates outward from your inner being, and nothing can disturb that peace—it *is* "all the same."

We are constantly judging and trying to assign meaning to everything in our experience: every event, every object, every interaction, every person, and everything we can see, hear, taste, and touch. We are meaning-makers by nature. If we could go through life without judging those around us or the circumstances of others, we would find ourselves happy and free.

There is a story of a Zen master who lived in a small village. He had many students and was well-thought-of in the community. One day one of his young students became pregnant. Her parents were furious and wanted to know who the father was. She was afraid to tell them, but finally, after pressure from her father, she told them it was the Zen Master. Her father immediately ran to the temple to confront the Master.

"You are a dirty scoundrel," he said. "You got our daughter pregnant, you're not a Master at all!"

The Zen Master simply replied, "Is that so?"

The irate father was appalled at the Master's serenity in the face of such a scandal. "Is that all you have to say for yourself?" he shouted. "You can rot here in your temple all alone. By the time I tell everyone what kind of person you are, you will have no more students!"

The girl's father told all the townspeople what the Zen Master had done, and one by one, his students left, saying they couldn't study with someone who had such low morals. In those instances where a student or townsperson confronted him and told him how terrible he was, his only reply was, "Is that so?"

With his students gone, the Zen Master continued to practice meditation and mindfulness and to care for his garden. His inner peace was unaffected by the opinions of others. A few months later, the father and daughter showed up on his doorstep with a baby. The Zen master greeted them and smiled at the girl and the small child. The girl looked down, ashamed.

The girl's father handed the child to the Zen Master saying, "This is your child, and now you will have to raise him."

The Zen Master gently took the child in his arms and replied simply, "Is that so?" and for the next year, he raised the child as if he were his own.

In the meantime, the girl's family was miserable. Her father was constantly feuding with his neighbor, the local butcher. He had forbidden his daughter from ever seeing the butcher's son, with whom she was madly in love. She finally broke down one day and, in a shower of tears, told her mother and father the truth: the child belonged to the butcher's son. Because their families hated each other so much and were always fighting, she had been afraid to tell them.

The next day the Zen Master heard a knock at the temple door. He picked up the child, who had now learned to walk and to occasionally sit quietly on the Zen Master's lap in meditation, and opened the door to see the humbled-looking father and daughter.

The father relayed the story to the Zen Master, and he and the young woman apologized profusely for all of the problems they had caused him. The girl's father took the child and said to the Zen Master, "You are a great person

and a true Master. This community is lucky to have someone such as you to teach us 'The Way.'"

The Zen Master replied simply, "Is that so?"

My father used to say, "Don't believe anything you
hear and only half of what you see." I didn't understand
that when I was young, but as I've grown older, life experience has taught me that we seldom know the whole story
about anything. I've learned to take the things people say
about others with a grain of salt. You can tell a lot about
someone who is venomously condemning or looking down
upon someone else.

Practice: The moment you catch your mind judging someone for something they are doing that doesn't seem to fit
into your value system, or your current model of the world,
try to remember a time or circumstance in which you did
something that you wouldn't agree with now. Just as we are
always growing and learning, so is everyone else around us.
Try to see people and circumstances as they are, without
looking through the colored lens of the ego. You never
truly know the whole story.

The flower doesn't spin or toil
Nor does it try to be anything
But a beautiful flower
Its fragrance travels on the breeze
Its beauty brings us to our knees

A tree doesn't worry or fret
Nor does it try to be anything but a tree
It stands tall, calm, and serene
Providing shelter and shade to those in need.

A human being
Is constantly judging

"This must mean that"
"That must mean this"
Weighing and measuring
With every thought

Forgetting we are human beings
Not human doings

Take a break from judging
We don't have to know
We don't have to judge

"This" may not mean "that"
"That" may not mean "this"
It is as it is
Why add to it?

In judging, we are judged
In weighing, we are weighed
In measuring, we are measured

Judge not
Weigh not
Measure not
Just be.

Anger

Anger is like a storm rising up from the bottom of your consciousness. When you feel it coming, turn your focus to your breath.

—THICH NHAT HANH

You will not be punished for your anger; you will be punished by your anger.

—BUDDHA

I'VE HAD A LOT OF PERSONAL EXPERIENCE WITH ANGER and overcoming anger. My father was an angry person. It seemed like a day wouldn't go by without him blowing up at someone for something seemingly insignificant. As a child, I watched him struggle with it. I don't know what his internal process or formula for anger was; I just remember his short fuse and explosive temper. He would seem enraged one minute, and in the next, his rage would be gone and almost forgotten—forgotten by him, at least. His

69

anger often left a lasting effect on many of us who were on the receiving end of his temper. It was the same with my father's parents. My mother recalls a time when my father and my grandmother were yelling at each other in our kitchen. My mother said they were arguing over whether Grandma had ever bought him a new pair of shoes when he was young. They were in a heated shouting match one minute, and in the next, my father said in a calm voice, "I think I'm going to have a cup of coffee. Ma, would you like one?" And my grandmother replied, just as calmly, "I believe I would, Bob." Just like that, over and forgotten.

My father was quick to anger, his parents were quick to anger, and it's probable that his grandparents were angry. I don't believe we have to be a product of our environment, but there is no doubt that the behaviors we see and experience on a daily basis shape the challenges we have to overcome as adults. And it's our responsibility to overcome those challenges and to break the cycle, for our children and loved ones as well as for our parents and ancestors. We can be the linchpin. We can become the healing element. But first, we must learn how, and then we need to make an unwavering effort.

Practice: When anger starts to rise within you, bring your attention to where the feeling is in your body. There is a definite mind-body connection in anger. The next time you feel anger beginning to rise, allow yourself to become aware of this connection. What is your posture like? What is your breathing pattern? What disempowering questions about the situation are running through your mind? I was always slow to anger, but once the fire was stoked, it was hard to put out, and afterward, I felt sick and terrible inside. It would rise as a great heat inside my chest, and I would find myself asking all sorts of negative questions about whatever situation seemed to be its cause. That feeling is very close to fear, and in truth, anger is caused by a fear of death of the ego, death of "my position" or "my beliefs about something." Just recognizing and observing this mind-body connection, and anger's basis in fear will help to break the pattern.

When dealing with the anger of others, we must learn to listen compassionately and to be like water. Water absorbs force. It doesn't resist. Listen for the intention behind the words. What is the angry person afraid of? What limiting beliefs and values might be the underlying cause of their anger? What negative questions might they be asking themselves about the situation?

I've found that when someone around us is angry, if we can remain calm and listen deeply, eventually we become like a mirror in which they begin to see their own reflection. Very few people like the way they look when they are angry. If you've ever been angry and then gone and looked in the mirror, you may have started laughing at yourself and the ugly faces you were making. This caused an immediate physiological change, and your anger subsided. Similarly, someone who sees their anger reflected in your calm and peaceful presence will lose the ability to be angry any longer.

The storm rages
Powerful waves crash against the cliff
The cliff doesn't shy away

Through thunder and lighting
And the pounding of the ocean
The cliff stands tall

The storm rages on
Tearing at the rocks
The cliff is immovable

In the morning
The cliff shines golden in the glowing sun
The ocean is calm and peaceful
The cliff is the same

Beautiful doves
Nestled into the caves of the cliff
Sheltered from the storm

Fly out and soar into the morning sky
Singing songs of joy for the new day

Be the cliff
Shelter your peace from the storm of anger
When it subsides
Let your doves of love and wisdom soar.

Nonviolence

*Nonviolence is not a garment to be put on and off at
will. Its seat is in the heart, and it must be an insepa-
rable part of our being.*

—MAHATMA GANDHI

BUDDHISTS AND HINDUS CALL THE PRACTICE OF NONVI-
olence *Ahimsa*. Ahimsa is not just refraining from physical
violence but from violent thoughts as well. In the 2500
years since Siddhartha Gautama became enlightened and
was named Shakyamuni Buddha, not one drop of blood
has been shed in converting people to Buddhism. Yet there
are over 500 million practicing Buddhists today. Mahatma Gandhi liberated a nation with nonviolence. On the
night he was arrested by a crowd of men with weapons and
swords, Jesus told his disciples to put away their swords—
that to live by the sword is to die by the sword.

We are all an expression of Being, the One-Self, or
God. When we finally awaken to recognizing ourselves

in all beings, violence is impossible. The only thing that separates us is our ego. When you are present and have transcended the egoic mind, you feel at one with all things. In that presence, someone would no sooner harm another life than they would harm themselves.

Practice: When you find yourself in a busy place, imagine you can feel the hum and energy of the other people and the vibrating activity of their minds. Now, imagine you can feel your deep connection to the One Being within us all and that you and everyone around you is an expression of that One Being.

The next time you are confronted with ignorance, try and remember that it's the ignorance of the ego and the delusion of the mind. Hidden underneath these is a perfect being whose light is being obscured. When you have realized this, and someone approaches you in need, you will care for them as you would care for yourself or your own children. Mother Teresa realized this. She was a mother of anyone in need, a mother to the world.

Fear leads to anger and division
Anger is fear of the death of the ego
"Me" and "my"
My opinion, my beliefs

My religion, my country, my race
My team, my family, myself

Here's the line
My circle of love
Unfortunately, you happen to be on the other side

Destroy the line
Expand your circle
To include all human beings
All of God's creation
And no violence will be possible.

War

Hatred has never been destroyed by hatred, but by kindness; this is the eternal law.

—BUDDHA

I object to violence because when it appears to do good, the good is only temporary; the evil that it does is permanent.

—MAHATMA GANDHI

What difference does it make to the dead, the orphans, and the homeless whether the mad destruction is wrought under the name of Totalitarianism or the Holy name of Liberty or Democracy?

—MAHATMA GANDHI

PEOPLE WEREN'T MEANT TO HARM EACH OTHER. ONE OF the most important commandments received by Moses was *Thou shalt not kill*.

Jesus said that not only should we not kill, but that we shouldn't even get angry or pass judgment.

When our children are sent off to war and put in life-or-death situations where they may have to kill or be killed, many of them end up coming back with post-traumatic stress disorder (PTSD)—if they even come back at all. We have lost more of our veterans to suicide than soldiers were lost in the Vietnam war.

My father was a highly decorated Marine and a Korean War veteran. He never wanted any of his children to take part in war. He used alcohol to deal with his nightmares and PTSD. During war, men, women, and children are killed or broken, countries are ravaged, children become orphans, and societies are decimated—many times for profit, and almost always out of ignorance.

Our young men and women become the living victims of war. They return home with nightmares and challenges, often struggling to reintegrate into society. They try to become good husbands, wives, fathers, and mothers again, and most of them find a way, but many are unable to.

My heart goes out to these young men and women, and their families, and I pray that they can someday see through the darkness and nightmares to the light and divinity inside of them and that it will shine through with a cleansing love and peace.

As a young man, I remember trying to understand why my father spent so much time sad and angry, and seemingly still on a battlefield, when he had been home for decades. The following are some of the lyrics to a song I wrote at age twenty about my father, shortly after his untimely death:

He was eighteen
Barely a man
When they told him he had to fight
It was time to take a stand

Taken from his home
And given a gun
Sent off to a foreign land
To kill his fellow man

The rain and the mud
Turned to rivers of blood
As death and survival
Became one

His only friend who didn't die
Was the one he cared for the least
His gun
And the voices said

C'mon, boy, take a stand
Fight for your country; you know you can
Kill your fellow man
In the name of God

C'mon, boy, take a stand,
Fight for your country; you know you can
Kill your brother
In the name of God.

Death

...Do not fear those who kill the body
but cannot kill the soul.
—MATTHEW 10:28

The eternal self is never born, and will never die. It
did not spring from anything, nor did anything spring
from it. This ancient one is unborn, eternal, everlast-
ing. It is not slain, even though the body is slain. If the
slayer thinks that he slays, or if the slain thinks that he
is slain, both of these know not. For the self can neither
slay nor be slain.
—THE KATHA UPANISHAD, PART 2:18–19

Don't cry for the dead.
Cry for the living who feel they've been left behind,
or who believe their loved one is lost forever.

ONE NIGHT, WHEN MY CHILDREN WERE YOUNG, I WAS sitting in the living room, reading a book, and I heard little footsteps coming down the stairs. I had put my daughter to bed sometime earlier, but it seemed she was still awake.

She climbed into my lap, and I asked her, "Why aren't you sleeping, sweetie?"

She replied, "Daddy, I'm scared."

"What are you scared of?" I asked.

"I can't stop thinking about Grandpa."

Her great-grandfather had passed away the day before. She was concerned about death. I told her there was no such thing as death.

"Your great-grandfather's body was old and worn out. He was tired and in a lot of pain. He was suffering. His body may have fallen down, but when he stood up again, he was shining brightly. Imagine that picture you've seen of him, when he was a younger, more handsome, and healthier man, and had just married your great-grandmother. Now, imagine him smiling and surrounded by a warm, glowing light. That's what he looks like now. Now, he's going to Heaven to wait for your great-grandmother, and your grandma and grandpa. That's how you can imagine him."

We talked a little more, and I carried her up to bed, sang her a song, and she drifted off to sleep.

He didn't have to wait long. His wife had stayed alive only long enough to care for him. She joined him a week later.

What I told my daughter wasn't just a story to ease a child's worry. This body is a vehicle, and when it's worn out or damaged beyond repair, our soul moves on.

When Jesus spoke of the kingdom of God, he said, *It is like unto leaven, which a woman took and hid in three measures of meal.* According to Eastern thought, the first measure is the causal body—or "idea body"—which is closest to the omnipresent One Being, God, Source, or Creator. The second measure is the astral body. Our astral body—or "subtle body," as it is sometimes referred to—is a body of light and vibration, shaped like a physical body but full of light, *made* of light. This body allows us to abide in the Astral Heavens. Which Heaven we are drawn to is dependent upon our beliefs, karma, thoughts, and vibrations. When our physical bodies die, we may be born again right away, or we may spend time in the astral realms between lives, continuing our learning, reuniting with family and friends who have gone before us, and waiting for our loved ones to join us.

The third measure is the physical body. This body allows us to interact with the physical world. Our attachment to it and its desires continues to draw us back to the physical realm over and over again until we transcend those desires and resolve our physical karma.

At the time of this writing, my mother is 86 years old. She has had such an amazing life that over the past six months, I've been interviewing and recording some of her life stories so that I might be able to better and more accurately tell them in the future. During one of these interviews she told me that just a few months after my father had died, she was sitting on the edge of her bed feeling tired and worn out. She was upset with him for leaving her at a time when all of their children were grown, and she and my father were looking forward to relaxing, traveling, and spending more time together. Exhausted, and lost in these thoughts, she looked over, and my father was sitting in the chair in their room, just a few feet away. He was shining with an incredible light.

My mother said, "He looked amazing and was sparkling. It was him, but I've never seen him with such a wonderful and loving smile on his face."

He stood up and said, "You are so beautiful."

She told me she remembered thinking, "Me? Beautiful?" and then thinking, "He must be looking directly into my soul."

He told her that he was sorry for everything and that he just wanted to see her one last time before he had to go.

He turned to leave, and she said, "Wait, take me with you."

He turned back to her, "What about the children? Do you really want to leave them?"

She knew she couldn't, and twenty-six years later, she's still here, giving advice to children and grandchildren and welcoming new great-grandchildren into the world.

The death of the body is not the end. Losing a loved one can be heartbreaking and seem devastating. But it's important for us to learn to embrace the suffering and let it run its course. There is a time to cry, a time to smile, and a time to laugh. We don't know what someone's purpose was in this life, or what they were here to learn and to teach in life and in death. When I say, "Don't cry for the dead," it's only to awaken within you the truth that there is no death.

Practice: Find a quiet place and sit or lie down in a comfortable position. Close your eyes and become aware of your breath. Feel each inhalation and exhalation as your abdomen gently rises and falls, and the air passes in and out of your nostrils. Be aware of each inhalation and exhalation for a few moments, relaxing with each breath. Now become aware of your body. Relax each body part, starting with your toes, moving across your feet to your heels, then to your ankles, shins, and calves. Feel the underlying energy pulsating up through your body like a wave in the ocean as you move your attention upward through your knees and thighs, glutes and hips, back and abdomen. Imagine this energy as a warm and pulsating white light. Let it rise through your fingers, hands, wrists, arms, and back, and through your chest and shoulders. Now let it rise up your neck, face, and head. Feel it on your lips, eyes, and skin. If there is anywhere in the body you feel any tension at all, release it now. Feel the warmth and comfort of this beautiful white light pulsating within you and surrounding you. You are now aware of your energy body. This is the body of light underlying the physical body. You can become aware of this body anytime you choose. When the physical body wears out and passes to dust, as all things do, this is the body that remains.

Don't cry for the dead
For there is no death
Nothing of value is ever lost

Cry for the living
Those who miss their loved ones
Pray that they can still feel
Their loving presence

Pray that they can feel the light
And love still connecting them
They are here
These eyes just can't see them

True love is never lost
Your loved one lives on

Close your eyes
Imagine them close
Open your heart
See them in the Divine light

They are not in some far-off place
They are right here
Find your peace
Feel them in your heart

And at the end of this life
When you shed this body
Like an old, worn-out coat

Your soul will be free
To journey to the other shore
And you will be reunited
In joyous love and peace.

The Mind

The mind is a wonderful servant, but a terrible master.
—ANONYMOUS

WHAT WE ARE NOW IS THE RESULT OF OUR PAST thoughts and ways of thinking. Unfortunately, most people have no control over their thoughts. Their thoughts control them. They do not so much *think* as they are *thought*.

People walk around this world living in their minds, being controlled by random thoughts that come unbidden, or thoughts that have become habitual. Some of these thoughts become thought patterns: thoughts about what happened in the past or what someone did to them; worries about things that might happen in the future; make-believe conversations with people; make-believe movies being played over and over on the backdrop of the mind; visions of getting something they want or desire.

The mind also loves to create problems to solve, and fantasies to live in. It's been estimated that the average person has up to 70,000 thoughts per day, and 95 percent of them are the same ones they had yesterday.

In studying neurolinguistic programming, through the various mental exercises it offers, you can learn to change your thought patterns and internal experience. In learning different psychologies, you can learn to *use* the mind to *work on* the mind.

In meditation and mindfulness, you learn to transcend the mind and connect with the spirit. When you can do this, the mind calms and quiets. When you quiet and direct the mind, it becomes a wonderful servant.

The mind loves to be entertained and occupied. It goes this way and that. When people are at work, they often distract themselves with music, or spend time daydreaming about what they would rather be doing, or planning what they are going to do when they get off work. Their focus is divided.

Then, when they are with their family, they are thinking about work: things left undone, things they need to do, or are going to do tomorrow.

Some people's minds are so divided that they can't hold down a job. They think it's because the job isn't right for them, or they don't like their co-workers, or it's a matter of just having better things to do, but many times, it's because they have no control over their minds, and their mental focus is so divided that they really just can't be present at the job.

The mind can be divided multiple times, and the more it's divided, the less potent it is, and the more scattered the person becomes. A divided mind has a less positive impact on the world

When you have focus, you can accomplish anything. Your mind becomes a valuable servant, and you can begin to direct it toward any goal you want to achieve.

When scientists take scattered light, then focus and magnify it into a single beam, it creates a laser that can cut through almost any substance. When we take all the energy that we've been wasting on our scattered and divided thoughts and bring it to bear on focusing the mind, we create our own mental laser beam, capable of cutting through any obstacle to achieving and manifesting our Divine purpose.

Practice: Choose an activity in which you find yourself regularly engaged, one you may not entirely enjoy, or one you may wish to learn to enjoy. As you begin the activity or task, bring to your breath and body the part of your awareness that would usually be listening to music or daydreaming. Bring your attention to each movement involved in performing the task at hand. When your mind starts to wander, bring your attention back to the present moment. If you are mopping the floor, you may silently recite, "Breathing in, I am enjoying mopping the floor; breathing out I am smiling." Be present in the activity. If you are engaging with people, then fully engage with them. If your attention wanders, bring it back to the present. If judgments come in about what you are doing, or about the people you are engaged with, simply observe those judgments and let them go.

A Zen master once said, "The only reason we meditate is that we can't be present throughout the day." We practice meditation morning and evening to calm the mind and to make it easier to practice mindfulness throughout the day.

Look here!
Look there!
Remember this?
Remember that?

I can't believe he did that to me!
Can you believe that she is acting like that?

I wish I could be there
I wish I were like them

I'm so much better than you
I'm sure I'm not good enough

I wonder what's in my news feed
Or what's in so-and-so's story
Hey, everyone, check this out
I must be happy
Look at all I've achieved

That room is a mess
Those lines aren't clean

Obsessing to dysfunction
The mind runs here and there
And we follow

Tripping and stumbling
The whole way

Slow the mind
Observe its activity
But don't get caught up in it

Like soothing a frightened horse
It's okay, little mind, be still

Below the mind, there is a calm
A peace
A resonance

Find it; dive deep

When you pause to listen
You can hear it
Feel it and sense it
Beneath the activity of the mind
Peace, love and joy

Be here now.

PART II:

Spiritual Practice

Meditation

Be still and know that I am God.

—PSALMS 46:1

But thou, when thou prayest, enter into thy closet, and when thou hast shut thy door, pray to thy Father, which is in secret, and thy Father, which seeth in secret, shall reward thee openly.

—MATTHEW 6:6

The Self (formless God or Source) cannot be known by study of the Scriptures, nor by intellectual perception, nor by hearing frequent sermons or discourses. The self cannot be known by the unrighteous, who are not tranquil, whose minds are not at rest, and who do not meditate on him. They can never attain the Atman [the true self], even by great knowledge.

—THE KATHA UPANISHAD P2:23–24

Sometimes, when I talk to people about meditation, they say, "Oh, I can't meditate. Believe me, I've tried; my mind just wanders all over the place." This is common. The mind doesn't *want* to be quiet. It doesn't *want* us to be present and free from it. It wants to rule us—and it often does.

Nothing of lasting value is easy. Anything worth achieving takes daily effort—including mastering one's mind.

Create a space in your house that is only for meditation. Every home should have a space like this. If you don't have enough space to designate an entire room, find a corner somewhere to set up a small altar in.

On your altar, you might place a candle and a statue of your deity or a saint you gravitate towards, and a small picture of Christ, Krishna, Buddha, or Muhammad. What matters is that you set up your space in a way that aligns with your beliefs or religion. If you don't consider yourself religious, set it up in such a way that feels right and peaceful.

This is the place where you will start each day.

You can practice yoga or stretching before you sit if you'd like. This helps prepare your body to be relaxed and comfortable during meditation.

POSTURE

I like to sit cross-legged on the floor, on a small cushion. You can do this, or you can sit on the edge of a chair, or on a pillow, or just cross-legged on the floor. If you're in a wheelchair, that's a good place to sit, too. What's important is that your spine is erect (if it can be), your chin is slightly tucked in, and your tongue is lightly touching the roof of your mouth. Breathe in and out through your nose.

PRAYER

You can begin your meditation with your favorite prayer. If you don't have a favorite, find one you like that inspires you. There are so many to choose from. I begin by saying: *Heavenly Father, Divine Mother, Jesus Christ, Buddha, Bhagavan Krishna, Great Saints of all religions, I bow to you all. Let your love shine through me, and may I awaken your love in all hearts. Om, Peace, Amen.*

You can use whatever name you choose for God, Source, or Being, and the names of whichever saints resonate with you.

If there are other prayers you want to add, it's a good time and space to do so. If there is someone in your life who needs strength and love to get through a difficult time, you can pray for them and send them loving thoughts.

What's most important is the intention.

THE SINGLE EYE

Let thine eye be single,
and thy body will be filled with light.
—MATTHEW 6:22

Many meditation instructors teach their students to close their eyes and slightly raise their eyebrows, or to focus the attention of their closed eyes *between* the eyebrows—the space where, in Eastern thought, the third, or astral, eye resides. I remember a picture that used to hang in my mother's house, of Christ kneeling in prayer, with the Divine Light shining down upon Him, directly onto his forehead. With diligent practice, you will be able to see this light and be filled with its joy and peace.

THE TEN BREATHS

There are many different ways to begin calming the mind for meditation. One way is to observe your breath. I use a beaded bracelet I made to help count my breaths. I once spent some time in a Trappist monastery in contemplation. While I was there, they gave me a beautiful rosary. The beads were made of olive wood from a tree in Bethlehem. At some point, the rosary fell apart, and I used the beads to make bracelets for my children and myself. The larger, olive-wood beads make up nine beads on my bracelet, to mark nine breaths; the smaller beads in between came from a bracelet given to me by a Buddhist monk. On each bracelet is a small lobster claw hook from which to hang a pendant that marks the tenth breath. We've had at various times pendants with an image of Saint Michael, an "OM" symbol, and even a small silver turtle there to remind its wearer to slow down and breathe.

Bring your awareness to your breath. Breathe in through the nose for a count of five. Hold for seven. Exhale through the nose for ten. This is one round. If you use a bracelet or beaded necklace, hold the first bead between your thumb and forefinger, inhale, hold, then exhale and move to the next bead before inhaling again. This will give you a slight pause between your exhalation and your next inhalation. Repeat this breath nine more times.

I do this exercise when I begin to meditate, and at least three other times throughout the day.

THE SIXTEEN BREATHS
OF AWARENESS

I used to practice this exercise, which Buddha taught his disciples every day, sometimes two or three times a day. It helps clear the mind and bring about inner peace. You may want to begin your meditation with the Ten Breaths (described above), followed by this exercise.

As you breathe each breath, mentally recite the following, with your focus and intention on the words and their meaning:

1. *Breathing in, I am aware that I am breathing in a long breath. Breathing out, I am aware that I am breathing out a long breath.*

2. *Breathing in, I am aware that I am breathing in a short breath. Breathing out, I am aware that I am breathing out a short breath.*

3. *Breathing in, I am aware of my whole body. Breathing out, I am aware of my whole body.*

4. *Breathing in, I am making my whole body relaxed and at peace. Breathing out, I am making my whole body relaxed and at peace.*

5. *Breathing in, I am happy. Breathing out, I am happy.*

6. *Breathing in, I am feeling Joy. Breathing out, I am feeling Joy.*

7. *Breathing in, I am aware of the activities of the mind in me. Breathing out, I am aware of the activities of the mind in me.*

8. *Breathing in, I am making the activities of the mind in me calm and peaceful. Breathing out, I am making the activities of the mind in me calm and peaceful.*

9. *Breathing in, I am aware of the mind. Breathing out, I am aware of the mind.*

10. *Breathing in, I am making the mind calm and peaceful. Breathing out, I am making the mind calm and peaceful.*

11. *Breathing in, I am focusing the mind. Breathing out, I am focusing the mind.*

12. *Breathing in, I am freeing the mind. Breathing out, I am freeing the mind.*

13. *Breathing in, I am observing the impermanence of all dharmas. Breathing out, I am observing the impermanence of all dharmas.*

14. *Breathing in, I am observing the fading of all dharmas. Breathing out, I am observing the fading of all dharmas.*

15. *Breathing in, I am contemplating Liberation. Breathing out, I am contemplating Liberation.*

16. *Breathing in, I am contemplating letting go. Breathing out, I am contemplating letting go.*

At this point, you may have found that your mind is calm, and you may just want to sit in silence and observe your breath for 5–15 minutes or more.

YOUR MANTRA

It's important to have a mantra to help calm and focus the mind during meditation. Your mantra could be a name for God, or a name like Jesus, Christ, Rama, Krishna, Buddha, or Muhammad. Or, it could be a mantra like *Om Mani Padme Hum* or *Sat Chit Ananda*. If you're Christian, you might use the mantra *Om Christave Namaha*, which means "Salutations to Christ" or "Bowing to Christ in the cosmic vibration of the Holy Ghost." Whatever your mantra, it should be short, and something you can easily recite in your mind while driving or waiting in line, or when you encounter a potentially stressful situation. It should be something that elevates your consciousness. You can also recite your mantra if you're afraid, worried, or having incessant or habitual thoughts about something. Mahatma Gandhi was fearful as a child, and he was taught by his Nana to recite *Rama* over and over to chase away the fear.

While I'm driving, I often just breathe and am aware of my breath while silently reciting *Om Mani Padme Hum*, which roughly means that God, Source, or the Cosmic Vibration is transforming the body, mind, and speech into altruistic, compassionate wisdom. It calms the mind and brings peace to the body and speech.

MEDITATION ON A PASSAGE OR PRAYER

Depending on the amount of time you have set aside to meditate, you can add or substitute meditating on a passage or prayer. Pick your favorite psalm or prayer, and slowly recite it over and over in your mind. Focus on each word with the power of your enhanced attention. You could recite something like the following prayer of St. Francis:

Lord, make me an instrument of Your peace
Where there is hatred, let me sow love
Where there is injury, pardon
Where there is doubt, Faith
Where there is despair, Hope
Where there is darkness, Light
And where there is sadness, Joy
O Divine Master, grant that I might not seek so much to be consoled as to console
To be understood as to understand
To be loved as to love
For it is in giving that we receive
It is in pardoning that we are pardoned
And it is in dying that we are born to eternal life.
Om, Peace, Amen

Recite your prayer very slowly over and over in your mind with intention. When your mind begins to wander, gently bring it back. At some point, you may find that the prayer is reciting itself, and you will begin to feel a great peace and expansion in your heart. When the prayer and your thoughts completely disappear, you have entered into *silent illumination*.

We are what we think about, and as things come up throughout the day, your prayer will begin to resurface and guide you toward what action to take.

EXPANDING THE SELF TO INFINITY

The following is an exercise that can help expand your consciousness during meditation:

1. Silently say to yourself, *I am not in this body; this body is in me*, and imagine expanding your consciousness equally in all directions to include your body.

2. *I am not in this room; this room is in me.* Now, the room and the body are inside you.

3. *I am not in this house; this house is in me.* Expand your consciousness to include the house or building.

4. *I am not in this city; this city is in me.* Continue expanding your consciousness.

5. *I am not in this world; this world is in me.* Imagine the entire earth is in you.

6. *I am not in this solar system; this solar system is in me.* Expand your consciousness to include the Sun, planets, and space.

7. *I am not in the cosmos; the cosmos is in me.* Imagine the entire cosmos is in you: billions of stars, planets, and infinite space.

Now, just be. Connect to the timeless and endless peace that underlies and encompasses all of creation.

SILENT ILLUMINATION

Be aware of your breath. Follow it in and follow it out. If any thoughts enter, simply view them as you would view a passing cloud and give no energy to them.

Smile. Feel the peace and love welling up from within, through your heart, surrounding you and enveloping you, permeating your being. Sit silently with no thought, engulfed in this peace. This silent illumination can come from the practice of any meditation technique. When the technique disappears and you enter that timeless and eternal space, the technique is working and has served its ultimate purpose.

BREATH AWARENESS ALL DAY

Not only does breath awareness help us to be calm, centered, and present, there is a direct correlation between our respiratory rate and our health and longevity.

A rabbit's respiration rate is thirty to sixty breaths per minute, and his life expectancy is only one to two years. Compare that to a tortoise, who only takes three to four breaths per minute and can live up to 250 years. The slow and steady tortoise wins every time.

Try having a part of your awareness on your breath all day. When your mind wanders, bring it back to your breath. Some of the most enlightening experiences will come from this exercise. When part of your awareness is always on your breath, your breathing becomes slow and measured, and you are brought back to the reality of the present moment. Energy and focus that is usually wasted on incessant and unnecessary thoughts is instead focused on the here and now. Your consciousness will expand. You will feel a deeper connection with, and a greater understanding of all people and things around you. The amount of yourself you will be able to give and share will multiply immensely.

This isn't easy, but it's not impossible—unless you never try it. Not attempting to practice is like hoping and praying to win the lottery without ever buying a ticket.

The first prolonged and profound breath awareness experience I can remember lasted about six hours. My wife and I had traveled to Lincoln, Nebraska, where we watched my oldest son play in a soccer game. The game ended late, so we decided to stay the night in a hotel before traveling home the following day. After we woke up, I had a nice meditation, and then we went to breakfast. Looking at the map on my phone, we found that the Lauritzen Botanical Gardens was on the way home, so we decided to visit. My wife loves flowers, plants, and trees, and spending time in nature is something we try to do as often as we can.

My wife wanted to drive, so I sat in the passenger seat, and began practicing the ten breaths. From there, I went into the sixteen breaths of awareness. My inner consciousness expanded and became more focused at the same time. I was able to leave part of my attention on every inhalation and exhalation as we traveled to the gardens, parked the car, and walked to the entrance.

As we bought the tickets and interacted with the woman at the reception desk, I was completely present, with part of my awareness on my breath. We visited the bathroom, and then browsed the gift shop. It felt as if everything was new and wondrous. I picked things up to look at them and saw them without judgment.

As we walked through the gardens, I felt a joyous expansion of the heart and a sense of oneness with all the beautiful plants, flowers, and trees. My wife and I held hands and talked about the things we saw. All the while, part of my attention was on my breath. I felt a closeness to the people we passed, and like witnessing the still waters of a pond, I had truly become the observer of my now calm and peaceful mind. We sat at a bench beside a pool, near the edge of the woods. A little stream poured into it from above.

After some time had passed, we decided to go eat in the cafeteria. We had a nice conversation with the woman who was working at the checkout. It's hard to describe the love and connection you feel for people—even complete strangers—when you are in this state of presence. Each conversation and interaction, each moment is the most important you will ever have.

We ate in presence, and then browsed the gift shop again. I drove the rest of the trip, maintained breath awareness, and remained in this beautiful state of Oneness during the two-hour ride home. When we arrived at our house, I dropped off my wife and drove to pick up my daughters at school. The only time my breath awareness slipped a little was when my daughters were fighting over who was going to be in charge of the radio. It was very brief, and part of my awareness was easily brought back to my breath.

I maintained the awareness even through a phone conversation in which my lead project manager and estimator at work told me he would be leaving the company in two days. In that state of Oneness, the news didn't bother me. I knew things were as they should be, and everything would work out for the best.

I would like to tell you that I remained in that state and never left, but you already know it lasted for about six hours. The state comes and goes; sometimes, it's very deep, and sometimes, it's just below the surface. Breath awareness is a good way to open the doorway. But most of the time, the mind doesn't want to obey our request to focus on something in the present moment. That's why we have to practice every day. The more we practice, the easier it becomes.

Some days may be blissful, and some days may be a struggle. Start meditating for twenty or thirty minutes a day, and as you become more comfortable, you can add more time. It may be helpful to use a timer with nice bells or chimes. Some meditation timers allow you to set interval bells. These are useful if you want to sit for a certain amount of time, but you also want to make sure you allow for silent meditation toward the end of your session.

Never give up. Organize your day and your life around your practice. What could be more important in this life than developing spiritually and discovering your true nature? If you practice daily, you will reach a point where your mind appreciates the break it receives during meditation, and you will sincerely look forward to it.

Meditation has been scientifically proven to be good for your mind and body; it's good not only for you but also for those around you as well. Everyone in your life will benefit from your calm and centered presence.

The only way to truly connect with God, Source, or Being is through meditation, prayer, and mindfulness. However, if it were easy, everyone would be doing it.

God said, through the divine incarnation of Krishna: *One in every thousand seek Me, and only one out of every thousand who seek Me find Me.* Be diligent. Every ounce of spiritual development you accumulate in this lifetime will be carried into the next.

I sat in silence
Yet heard a grand symphony

I sat in darkness
Yet basked in a light
brighter than ten thousand candles

The room was cold
Yet I was filled
with the warmth of a raging fire

I was alone
Yet was embraced by a love
greater than that of a mother for her newborn child

The room was small
Yet my spirit soared to infinity

I was nothing
Yet became a part of everything.

PART III:

Your Life's Purpose

Desire

Underlying every desire is the desire to know and to reconnect with our true nature.

THE WORD *DESIRE* COMES FROM THE LATIN, *DE SIDERE*, which means "from the stars" or "of the heavens." The Heavenly Father and Divine Mother gave us the desire to know Them, but we have forgotten how. We don't even realize that we need or want to know Them. The few of us who attempt it come back empty-handed or settle for some sort of empty, emotional high—a high brought about not by direct experience, but by an inspiring sermon or a potential misinterpretation of scripture. Emotional highs fade and are often followed by emotional lows.

Even the atheist is driven by the desire to know and reconnect with the source of all life. The desire for wealth, material things, sex, alcohol, drugs, power, adventure, and distraction are all insatiable. They will never fill the void created by our disconnect from the omniscient "I Am."

Are you ever completely satisfied and at peace? Or do you feel like you are constantly chasing after something unattainable? Do you often feel like there's something missing in your life?

It's been said we are Divine Beings, having a human experience. And we *are* Divine Beings, suffering from amnesia. We are the Lion that has been raised with the sheep since birth and thinks he is a sheep. So, instead of claiming our birthright of everlasting love, peace, and prosperity *now*, we instead chase sensory pleasures and make-believe goals, hoping they will fill the void that has been left by our disconnection with the source that underlies all creation.

You may think: *When I get that new car, I will be happy.* Then you get the new car, and you are excited about it for a few days or weeks, but the newness fades, and you're on to the next thing. Maybe it's a new pair of shoes or a smartwatch or the newest iPhone or a big promotion at work. We go on and on and on, chasing desire like a mouse running on its wheel.

Occasionally, something happens, and our mind slows down and stops. We have a peaceful moment. It could happen during a walk through the woods, or by the ocean, or while just sitting quietly on your porch in the morning light. The mind quiets, and we feel an expansion of the heart. Then the neighbor's dog starts barking, and the judgment and irritation reel starts rolling, and it's back on the wheel again.

What we don't realize is that inner peace is our natural state, and with a little self-scrutiny and practice, we can liberate ourselves from desires that no longer serve us, and instead bring clarity and purpose to our lives.

Practice: Observe your desires. Ask yourself, "When I get or achieve or become ____, what will that do for me?" When you have the answer, ask yourself, "And what will *that* do for me?" Keep drilling down and asking yourself that question over and over until you're at the final answer, which is usually something like, "Well, it will make me feel good," or "It will make me happy," or "It will make me feel free." All that chasing, just to find something that can truly only come from within, something you can have all the time *right now*.

Jesus said, *The Kingdom of God is within you. Seek ye first the Kingdom of Heaven, and all the rest will be added unto you.* Seek the joy and happiness within; then you can share it and experience it without. When you have the joy and happiness that comes from inside, your desires become selfless. You are already full. When you are full, you are no longer looking for what you can get but for what you can give. You are no longer seeking to be consoled but to console, and are no longer seeking to be loved but to love.

Don't chase after happiness in the storm of desire
Even the blind can see the futility
Seek your connection first to the peace within
Find it, and when you walk into the world
Bring it with you
Hold it high
Like a light on the end of a candlestick
Dispelling the darkness and delusion

Bring your peace to the world
Shine your inner light into every situation
Share it with your family
Spread it in your work
Shine it upon every stranger you meet

Don't expect to gain inner peace and joy
From anything outside of yourself
Uncover the inner peace and joy
That is your true nature
And share it with the world.

Suffering

*If there is a meaning in life at all, then there must be
a meaning in suffering. Suffering is an ineradicable
part of life, even as fate and death. Without suffering
and death, human life cannot be complete…Everything
can be taken from a man but one thing: the last of the
human freedoms—to choose one's attitude in any given
set of circumstances, to choose one's own way.*
—VICTOR E. FRANKL, *MAN'S SEARCH FOR MEANING*

DESIRE AND SUFFERING ARE TWO SIDES OF THE SAME
coin. We suffer when we don't achieve the things we desire,
and we suffer when we do achieve them, and they are later
lost or taken from us. We suffer when we achieve our
desire, and yet are unable to find the peace and joy in it
that we had hoped it would bring.

Suffering and unhappiness arise when our life conditions don't equal our life expectations. You may have
expected to be happily married by now. You may have

expected to get that big raise or promotion. You may have expected vibrant health and are now experiencing fatigue or disease. You may have expectations of the people in your life, and they seem to be falling short.

Victor Frankl didn't expect to lose his family and all of his possessions when he was taken to the Nazi concentration camps. He and the survivors of those camps were living proof that one has the freedom to "choose one's attitude in any given set of circumstances, to choose one's own way." In *Man's Search for Meaning*, he wrote about how many of the people who were able to survive those camps developed an empowering meaning for their suffering and circumstances. They were stripped of literally everything except their freedom to choose the way in which they responded to their circumstances.

Mr. Frankl went on to create Logotherapy, a school of psychotherapy built upon the belief that finding meaning in life, and in any experience, is the most powerful driving force in human beings. We are meaning-makers. The question we need to ask ourselves is: Will the meaning we find for our life circumstances be an empowering, or a disempowering meaning? Just realizing that we have a choice can sometimes be enough to liberate us from disempowering meanings and beliefs.

Gerald Coffee wrote a book called *Beyond Survival* about his seven-year experience as a POW during the Vietnam War. He was chained to a bed in a tiny cell, barely fed, and beaten every day. In an interview, I heard him say that he wouldn't take back the experience even if he could. During that time as a prisoner, he learned just how powerful the human spirit is. He did pushups and sit-ups in his cell every day and in his mind, played eighteen holes of golf. He relived every birthday, holiday and Christmas. As his body was confined and beaten down, his spirit grew. Knowing that his captors were soldiers with families, doing what they were forced to do, he forgave them, in a similar way that Victor Frankl forgave his captors. After Gerald Coffee was released and returned home, he went on to write his book about his experience and to speak in public about the power of the human spirit.

When our life conditions don't meet our life expectations, we have two choices. We can change either our life conditions or our life expectations. Neither Gerald Coffee nor Victor Frankl had the option of changing their life conditions, so they changed their life expectations and their attitude toward their suffering. They embraced their suffering with dignity and used the insights that they had gained from their experiences to help others.

Practice: What in life may be causing you suffering? How can you embrace it? Can you change your life circumstances? If not, how can you change your life expectations? What empowering meaning can you derive from your suffering? To live is to suffer. It's human nature. It's in how we suffer and in how we overcome our suffering that matters most.

Victor Frankl said there were two types of suffering: the first is brought about by outside forces beyond our control, such as being ill, or imprisoned in a concentration camp; and the second is self-inflicted, brought about by poor focus and lack of meaning. You may think, "How does my suffering compare to that of someone who has been in a concentration camp, or who has been a prisoner of war, or who is dying of a terminal illness?"

Victor Frankl said that a person's suffering is like a gas that fills a room. It doesn't matter the degree or type of suffering; it still fills the room.

I challenge you to break a window or open a door in the room of your suffering and let in the fresh air of illumination and freedom. If your suffering is self-inflicted, find a way to let it go. If your suffering is not self-inflicted, try to find an empowering meaning in it.

Gandhi arose from the
Suffering of a nation

Martin Luther King, Jr.
From the suffering of a race

Mother Teresa from the
Suffering of the sick and poor

Buddha from the
Suffering of humanity

Christ from the
Suffering of the world

The Phoenix rises from the
Flames of suffering

Let your suffering burn away
All that is unreal
So, all that remains is
The power, love and light of
The true self.

Nonattachment

*Lay not up for yourselves treasures (attachments) upon
Earth where moth and rust doth corrupt, and where
thieves break through and steal. But lay up for yourselves treasures in Heaven, (the Kingdom of Heaven
within) where neither moth nor rust doth corrupt,
and where thieves do not break through nor steal. For
where your treasure (your attachment) is,
there will your heart be also.*

—MATTHEW 6:19–21

*When all desires dwelling in the heart are renounced,
the mortal becomes immortal.
When all the ties of the heart are unraveled, the
mortal becomes immortal.*

—THE KATHA UPANISHAD

*It is easier for a camel to go through the eye of a needle
than for a rich man to enter into the Kingdom
of Heaven.*

—MATTHEW 19:22

THE "RICH MAN" WHOM JESUS SPEAKS OF IN THE BOOK of Matthew is someone with great attachments, whose possessions and wealth aren't just tools to be used for the greater good, but have become an integral part of his identity. Conversely, a person who hasn't manifested material wealth in their lives can also have great attachments. If they take pride in being someone who is "above the pursuit of wealth" and see themselves as superior and more spiritual than those who have worked hard to attract material wealth into their lives, they have unwittingly become the "rich man." Their identity of being someone who is morally superior has become their greatest possession. The attachment to this identity will impede their spiritual development as surely as someone else's love for their new luxury car.

It's said that wealth only serves to magnify the personality that is already there. If you are ignorant, and you achieve or obtain wealth, you will have even more opportunities to be ignorant. If you are generous and kind, and you accumulate or obtain wealth, you will have even more opportunities to be generous and kind.

Some people are so caught up in wanting to appear wealthy that they will finance a big house, luxury vehicles, and toys they can't even afford. They have so little presence and inner peace that they are striving to appear to be "somebody," and they are looking for as much external validation as they can find.

I have a prosperous friend who takes 50 percent of everything he earns from one of his businesses and invests it into a leadership program he developed to help "at-risk" youth. His goal is to have one thousand kids in the program. The last time I spoke with him about it, he had 800 kids enrolled, and with the help of local business owners, he was teaching them to shake off the shackles of their environment and to become leaders. He has been doing this for a long time, and I knew him for years before he ever mentioned it to me. He may have accumulated some material wealth in his lifetime, but he is not the "rich man" of whom Jesus speaks.

Don't be attached to wealth and material possessions, and don't be attached to your identity as someone who is above material wealth. Sometimes, the latter path is one of laziness and fear of failure disguised as righteousness.

Practice: Make a list of the things you are attached to in your life—things that, if you lost them, would make you feel like you had lost a part of yourself or your identity. Your list could include material things, such as a house, car or a collection of some sort, family heirlooms, investments, properties, or just money in the bank. Add to the list your profession and any identities or roles you have adopted, voluntarily or (seemingly) involuntarily. Be exhaustive in this list. Who would you be without these things? What would remain?

Now, ask yourself how you can renounce these things—if not physically, then in spirit, so that they no longer own or define you.

When Buddha initiated a monk, the monk could only have three robes and a begging bowl. When Jesus took on a disciple, he told them to renounce the world. Most of us aren't monks; we have a purpose and obligations outside of the monastery. So how can you renounce your "great possessions," at least in spirit? As we observe in the Sixteen Breaths of Awareness, we never truly own anything. Every dharma is impermanent and eventually fades. What remains?

Don't believe your eyes
Don't believe your ears
Don't believe your touch
Don't believe your cravings
Don't believe your mind

It has been said that "God is a Spirit
We must worship Him in Spirit"

Direct your focus inward
Connect with the Spirit
Let that be your treasure
And all the rest will fade and be proven false

Speak the truth
Eat the truth
Drink the truth
Think only truth
Be the truth

Live the truth in every way
Then, you will know God.

Faith

You may have heard of the power of intention—
or "the secret." The truth is that there is no secret.
The Enlightened Ones have never tried to hide it.
It's faith, pure and simple.

JESUS SAID THAT IF YOU HAD THE FAITH OF A MUSTARD
seed, you could move a mountain, and that nothing would
be impossible for you. But what is the faith of a mustard
seed, and how do we learn to manifest it into our lives?

A mustard seed is tiny. It's only one or two millimeters in diameter. How could the faith of something so small contain so much power and potential? Ramban, a thirteenth-century Jewish philosopher, said that when the universe first appeared, it was no larger than a mustard seed, yet contained within it was everything it needed to expand and to manifest all of existence as we know it. A mustard seed has everything it needs within its tiny little stature to grow into one of the largest plants in the garden, and when the conditions are right, it will achieve this every time without a doubt. It simply does what it was created to do.

What is faith? Just as you know the sun will rise tomorrow, or that when you drop an apple, it will fall downward and not upward, you know in your heart, without a doubt, that something will happen or can be accomplished. This is faith.

God will take care of it, whatever it is, if you have faith. The Universe or Source will manifest your desire if you have faith.

I remember a time in my life when I was young and struggling financially. I had just filled out an application to rent my very first home. It was a beautiful little duplex in a quaint neighborhood, and I couldn't afford it, but I prayed and had faith that if I continued to do my part, God would take care of the rest. I had strong resolve. I thought: *I need this place, and God will take care of it.*

The landlady chose my application over the rest. I rented the duplex and made the rent payment month after month. Not many months later, I bought the whole property, remodeled it, and rented out the other unit.

Whatever the mind can conceive and believe,
it can achieve.
—NAPOLEON HILL

Once when I was in my mid-thirties, I herniated a disc in my neck while practicing Jiu Jitsu. I was in incredible pain. I couldn't move my right arm and had to wear it in a sling. After several medical appointments and an MRI, the doctors and surgeons were convinced that I would need to have my disc removed and the two vertebrae screwed and fused together in my neck. Not only would this have caused the range of motion in my neck to become severely limited, but it could have also resulted in many other problems and complications. I respectfully declined their treatment plan. I knew that the body was designed to heal itself and had faith that I could find a better way. I prayed for a more holistic and less intrusive solution.

A friend of mine, who was a grappling coach, told me about a chiropractor who had a Spine Med table and was having success with spinal decompression therapy. He thought that it might be helpful and gave me the doctor's name and number. I met with the doctor and found out that I was a good candidate for the procedure. I would need to travel to his office for twenty-one sessions to complete the process, and it wasn't covered by insurance. If it didn't work, I would be back to square one and looking at an archaic and invasive surgery. I had faith that it would work.

I drove an hour and a half to the doctor's office three days a week for the next three months. During each visit, I spent thirty minutes on the spinal decompression table with my head and neck strapped into it, followed by fifteen minutes of electrical stimulation and ice. The Spine Med machine was computerized and had been programmed to provide a certain amount of traction for a short duration and then to release and repeat.

Lying prone with my eyes closed three days a week allowed me ample time to visualize the healing process. I imagined the tear in my disc growing back together, my arm getting better, and the nerves growing back down into my thumb. I imagined practicing martial arts and yoga again, and having great range of motion in my neck. After three months of treatment, I felt much better, and within a year, I had regained complete range of motion in my neck, and the numbness down my arm and into my thumb had disappeared.

Another story of how faith and prayer changed my life came from a sincere prayer answered by our Divine Mother: I prayed for our Divine Mother to bring someone into my life who was compassionate, understanding, loving, and kind. I didn't just pray; I beseeched her from down on my knees with an aching heart and tears in my eyes. My prayer was heartfelt and sincere. Her love and light washed over me and filled me with a deep inner peace. I had complete faith that my prayer would be answered when it was meant to be. Not long after, I met the wonderful and compassionate woman who became my best friend, and later, my loving wife.

There are many more inspiring stories of faith in my life, and in the world. I believe most anyone can look at their life, or at the life of someone close to them, and find such stories.

Practice: The following is an adaptation of an NLP exercise I learned. Begin by sitting in a comfortable position and closing your eyes. Observe the inhalation and exhalation of your breath. As you begin to relax, think of something in your life that you truly desire—something about which you are currently uncertain. It could be as small as an opportunity coming into your life that you've been hoping for or as large as making a major career change. When you think of it, imagine what it looks like. Is the image close or far away? Is it bright or dim? Is it colorful or bleak? What are the sounds associated with it? What does it feel like in your body?

Now, imagine something that you're completely certain about, something in which you have complete faith. Is the image of this experience closer or further away than the uncertain one? Does it take up your full field of vision? Are the colors more vibrant, or dimmer? What does it sound like? How does viewing this image feel in your body?

After you've spent some time noticing the differences between the two scenes or images, go back to the first uncertain vision and change all of the modalities—size of the image, colors, vibrancy and richness of sound—so that they match, or are similar in mood and scope to the vision you are more certain about. If the uncertain image was far away, bring it closer. Turn up the vibrancy of the colors, adjust the sounds, make them richer and more immersive. Take all of the modalities from the vision you were certain about and overlay them onto the vision you were previously uncertain about. Notice the change in the way it feels in your body. Bathe the image in the cosmic light of the soul. Now feel the certainty that through faith and the power of intention, this desire, event, or circumstance will manifest itself into your life. Immerse yourself in this vision and see it as already done.

Faith comes from within
From your heart
From the source of all things manifest

Faith is indisputable
Beyond doubt
Faith can move mountains
Faith can feed and clothe the hungry thousands

Faith can build bridges
And liberate nations
Faith can overcome all barriers and obstacles

If you can for one moment
Remember who you truly are
There will be no more room for doubt
And all obstacles will be removed from your path

And YOU will become faith's instrument.

Intention

*Intention is a compelling vision, combined with
complete faith and belief in its fruition.*

WHEN YOU SET A GOAL AND VISUALIZE ITS FRUITION,
you're there at the finish line, and you can hear the crowd.
You feel everything you would feel having achieved your
goal. You can see everything you would see, hear everything you would hear, and know everything you would
know. You imagine the goal as if it's already been achieved.
When you believe it with strong faith, and you send it out
with the power of intention to the Universe, the Universe
has no choice but to send it back to you.

When you let your intention go and proceed to do the
work without any attachment to the outcome, the Universe will bend itself to fulfill your intention. The Universe
is like a mirror, reflecting your beliefs, focus, and desires
back to you. Everything you send out into the Universe
comes back to you. You will randomly meet people who are

aligned with your vision and are ready to help. Things will seem to fall magically into place.

This is a power we have and use, whether we like it or not; it is a force, like gravity. Everything we have and are experiencing in this moment, we consciously or unconsciously intended in the past. The thing we need to develop is the habit of consciously directing this power. That way, instead of experiencing the consequences of our previously unfocused and random thoughts and actions, we will manifest the things we truly want in our lives.

The most powerful intention is fueled by a higher purpose. When our intention is selfless, and its fruition will positively benefit others, the amount of assistance we can receive is limitless.

Practice: This is a slight variation on a valuable exercise I learned while studying with some of the pioneers of NLP (neuro-linguistic programming) during a thirty-day practitioner's certification program in Winter Park, Colorado.

Find a quiet place. Stand, look out before you, and imagine your goal in the distance (this could be ten or fifteen feet away, depending on how much room you have). Now, slowly walk on this newly-created timeline, realizing it is the trajectory to achieving your goal.

Feel it pulling you with a powerfully magnetic force connected to your heart. As you near the fruition of your goal and are taking your final step, know that you have achieved it.

Close your eyes and, as discussed earlier, see what you would see, feel what you would feel, and hear what you would hear when you have achieved your goal. Immerse yourself in it. Then, when you have faith that you are there, turn your head and look back along the timeline to where you started and see all the steps it took to get you there. What was the first step? The information will come to you. See each step, imagine everything you accomplished on the way, and write it down. You'll be amazed at the results.

Now that you've planted the seed, take action without fear or attachment to the outcome. Make the journey your destination. Don't live for the achievement of the goal; live for each day, marveling at how the world conspires to help you.

In the silence
That lies beyond the activities of the mind
Beyond thoughts and fears
Is a field of pure potential
A field from which all things manifest

Plant the seed of your intention there
And simply allow it to grow
Don't disturb the field

A tree doesn't need to be forced to grow
Everything that it requires
To begin its journey is in the seed
Just as the seed of your intention
Has everything it needs to manifest and flourish

The farmer doesn't worry
That the plants have forgotten how to grow
She doesn't go look at them ten times a day
She plants the seeds in fertile soil
And allows the sun and the rain
To perform their dharma

Plant your intention
In the fertile field of pure potential
In the peace and calm of meditation
And from that place of peace
Watch it grow and flourish.

Compassion

The great and compassionate heart is
the essence of enlightenment.
—GANDAVYUHA SUTRA

IN CH'AN BUDDHISM, ONE OF THE PRACTICES TO HELP alleviate suffering is compassion. There are four components of compassion. The first is understanding your internal conflicts and possessing inner peace. Jesus said, *First, cast out the beam that is in your own eye, and then, you will be able to see clearly enough to cast out the mote that is in your brother's eye.* To truly understand another's suffering, we have to acknowledge and understand our own. Having inner peace allows us to be an empty vessel without judgments. Then, we can move on to the second and third components of compassion, which are understanding the shortcomings of others, and forgiving them for their mistakes.

These lay the foundation for the fourth component of compassion, which is developing a deep and empathetic concern for the suffering of others. It's easy to say things like, "Well, it's their own fault," or "I have my own problems; there's nothing I can do to help them," and move on. But once we understand and develop the four components of compassion, our neighbor's suffering becomes our own.

Practice: Think of someone you know who is suffering. You may have thought their ignorance was the cause. In most cases, you would be right. Ignorance is the cause of all suffering, internal and external. It's also the cause of our inability or unwillingness to reach out to those around us who are suffering.

Try to understand where they are coming from. Imagine what their past must have been like for them to have developed the limiting beliefs that have kept them trapped in their current circumstance and mindset. From a place of understanding, we can develop the compassion we need to make a difference in the world.

Have compassion for those who are suffering
For those who are ignorant
For those who are blind
For those who are lost

As the Masters had compassion for us
Compassion enough to be reborn into this
Physical realm and suffer the birth and death of
The body again to help free us from our suffering.

Within every Being is the One Self
You are the Self
You are connected to all living beings
Their suffering is your suffering

See yourself in others' suffering
Make it your own
Shed light into their darkness
Sow love, faith and hope

You are the light of the world.

Family

*The problem with the world is that we draw
the circle of family too small.*

—MOTHER TERESA

FAMILY HELPS US LEARN TO LOVE UNCONDITIONALLY. I come from a very large family; I am the youngest of eight children. My mother and father taught us to stick together and to love and support one another. With a family as large as we have, there is a plethora of personalities, beliefs, and attitudes. Ideally, you learn to love your parents, brothers, sisters, cousins, aunts, uncles, nieces, and nephews—regardless of your differences. This is one of our circles of love.

Our family is a microcosm of our bigger family—the human race. When you can love and accept your family for who they are, and respect where each of them is on their spiritual journey, you can begin to expand that circle of love to include all of humanity.

When my children were little, I remember thinking: *These are God's children, and He has entrusted them into my care.* This understanding makes us more patient, loving and caring. If God came to you and said "I am going to send to you my children and I want you to care for them with patience, kindness and understanding. Each one will be different and will possess different talents and strengths. Love them unconditionally, nurture them, help them develop their talents, and teach them to lead a happy life"—what would you do? How would that change your attitude and beliefs about being a parent?

In essence, God has said this to all of us. We have been told many times that we are all children of God. What a privilege to raise the children of our Heavenly Father and Divine Mother. What a Joy to care for them when they are sick, to console them when they are sad, to comfort them when they wake up from a bad dream, and to work hard in the world in order to provide for them. There are no greater teachers of unconditional love than our children. They are truly from Heaven, and a blessing from God.

My wife and I and her parents recently spent a week in Hawaii on the island of Kauai. Everyone was researching and picking one thing they wanted to do while on our trip. My wife chose a kayaking adventure which ended in a hike to the bottom of a beautiful waterfall. When we go on vacation, I usually just enjoy doing what everyone else wants to. I can be content in just finding a used bookstore and perusing the spirituality section. My wife told me there was a Hindu monastery on the island. She knew visiting the monastery would be something special. I found their website and learned that if you were Hindu, you could schedule Darshan with Satguru Bodhinatha Veylanswami. I didn't think an illumined Guru would care if I was Hindu or not, so I emailed the monk in charge of scheduling and requested Darshan. I told him my wife and I practiced Kriya Yoga as taught by Paramahansa Prajnanananda. I received an immediate reply saying we could meet him on June 12 at 11am.

The temple and monastery are situated on 300 beautiful acres. The serenity we all felt upon arrival was palpable. My wife and I meditated in the temple while a monk performed a wonderful puja and mediation. It was peaceful and divine. We then joined her parents on the tour and were able to see the new temple that was under construction. We were able to witness Indian craftsman carving incredible statues and works of art out of granite with simple chisels and mallets.

As 11 o'clock approached, we made our way to our meeting with the Satguru. When we arrived, we both knelt before him and were struck by how gentle he was. He permeated a calm and gentle presence that surprised me. We talked about many things but the most important for me was what he had to say about family. He asked about my spiritual practice and I told him I meditated and practiced

Kriya Yoga most every morning and sometimes later in the day. I told him I tried to practice breath awareness and mindfulness throughout the day as well.

He said that was good and to continue to do so but to remember that I wasn't a monk and my most important duties were as a father and husband. He said, "Right now you have duties in the world. Continue to practice but don't ever feel like your children or family are interrupting your practice."

He said when my kids were grown and when my obligations were fewer, I would be able to dive deeper into the spirit. The gentle Guru stressed the importance of maintaining the habit of regular meditation now because when we get older it's easier to continue the habits we've developed than it is to make new ones. He reconfirmed my belief that every part of life is a spiritual journey and interacting with and nurturing your family and being present and loving in raising your children is as important as time spent in meditation and prayer.

Practice: Bring awareness to your relationships with your family. With your mother and father, aunts and uncles, sisters and brothers, stepparents and stepsiblings, with your spouse or significant other, and with your children. Are these relationships where you think they should be or where you would like them to be? Have you neglected these relationships because of challenges or grievances or because you live far away from each other? Try and learn to cultivate these relationships in a positive way. Make an effort to mend any broken relationships and to reaffirm neglected ones. If you've been abused or wronged by a family member in a way that makes reconciliation difficult or seemingly impossible, forgive them from afar and let them go.

When it comes to your spouse and children, make a commitment to put them first in your life. Be present in your interactions and take interest in the things that are important to them. Treat them with patience and loving-kindness. No major problems ever arose in a relationship based on selfless love and commitment.

Love and care for the children
That have been drawn into your life
Teach them to be honest and kind
Loving and patient

Teach them to work hard and to serve others
Lead them by example
Show them unconditional love

Say unto them,
"Beautiful child,

When you smile, the world shines brightly
When you laugh, it's the sound of joy
When you're sad, the world seems sad
When you cry, I want to wipe away your tears

Someday, you'll grow up
And will be out on your own
My greatest wish for you
Is that you'll never feel alone

Because any true love you've ever felt
Is never lost
It's always there, ever present
And inside your heart."

And pray:
"Heavenly Father, Divine Mother, let the beautiful children
That you've entrusted into my care always feel Your
Unconditional love, and may I be a conduit of that love and
Light."

Friends

And let there be no purpose in friendship,
save the deepening of the spirit.
—KAHLIL GIBRAN, *THE PROPHET*

True friendship is a blessing from the Divine. Shelter
and protect it as if it were a beautiful flower in a
thunderstorm.

LOVE THE WORLD AND CHERISH FRIENDSHIPS THAT ARE positive, loving, and supportive. Seek only friends of good morals and values who are interested in higher spiritual pursuits and selfless endeavors, until you are deeply rooted in love, faith, and your spiritual practice. These are the friends who will help you and accompany you along your spiritual journey. Although the dharma of your lives may not always allow you to spend a lot of time together, you will find your circles interconnecting from time to time, when they need to, bringing magic, synergy, and higher purpose to whichever endeavors you pursue.

Prior to attracting enlightened friendships, you may be progressing on your spiritual journey, while your old friends are not. They may still be more interested in swimming in the sea of desire and engaging in selfish pursuits. It's easy to want to keep these people in our lives out of habit and familiarity, and sometimes, out of a feeling of obligation. Give them a chance to join you on your journey. Offer them encouragement and guidance. If they are unwilling to accept it, if they are engaged in negative and selfish activities, or if they seek to try and drag you down, you must let them go their own way. Our friends don't want to lose us, and sometimes, that means they don't want to see us succeed, because it may mean leaving them behind.

My mother used to say, "Tell me who you hang out with, and I will tell you who you are." Although I didn't want to hear this wisdom as a teenager, there is a certain truth to it.

To realize the beauty of one's true nature is life's most important journey. Let your actions, speech, and character tell your life's story. The more you practice, and the more you grow, the more you will attract friends of similar values and character.

Sometimes, your character and dedication will inspire old friends, and they may want to join you on the path. But, a lot of the time, they won't. A few of them may even treat you with animosity and resentment. They may say something like, "Oh, so you think you're better than us?" Or, they may try to remind you of past transgressions to prove you aren't worthy of a life of spiritual pursuit. Don't let anyone pull you from your path. Pray for them. Send them love. But don't engage them on a negative level, even if it is something you may have done in the past.

Thomas Merton, a devout Trappist monk and one of the foremost spiritual writers of his time, wrote an essay entitled, "Thich Nhat Hanh is My Brother." These two spiritual seekers—one Christian and one Buddhist—exemplify the teachings of Christ and Buddha, and theirs was a friendship built on faith, love, and understanding. It was an example of an ideal friendship, one that transcends nationality and religion.

Help those in need and gather those people around you who are of good character, are seeking to better themselves, and have a desire to contribute to the greater good.

Practice: Take inventory of your friends. What is the nature of each of your friendships and how do you support each other? Foster those friendships which are sincere and supportive. We've all been in situations or have seen people in situations where they are constantly being taken advantage of under the guise of friendship. Be honest with yourself and let those people go who only seem to take from you but never want to contribute anything of value. If you've had a problem with alcohol or drugs, remove yourself from friends who only want to drink and do drugs. True friends will meet you at the coffee shop instead of at the bar. Friends who only want to gossip and speak badly of others will drop away when you no longer have any negativity to contribute. Eventually you may have fewer "friends," but you will have more true friends.

On a deeper level, when you are content with yourself, connected to your true nature and confident in who you are, you may find that everyone you meet is a friend.

Don't associate with those
Whose only story is "So-and-so did this to me
And so-and-so did that to me
All my problems are caused by so-and-so
Can you believe so-and-so?"

The more you hear it, the sorrier you begin to feel for "so-and-so"!

Only the fool associates with fools
True friends see your spiritual progress and say,
"How are you so happy and peaceful?
What are you reading? What are you studying?
What are you practicing? You're always so positive."

When you are truly established in your practice
You can help the ignorant
When you are truly present
Even a fool's hallucination begins to fade in your presence
We were all fools once

Always put on your oxygen mask first
Before putting on the oxygen mask of the
Person next to you
For you can only save someone else
If you have first saved yourself.

Dharma

The meaning of life is to find your gift.
The purpose of life is to give it away.
—PABLO PICASSO

THERE ARE MANY DEFINITIONS OF THE WORD *DHARMA*. One definition is that your dharma is your true calling or your life's purpose. It's what you were born to do in this life. You are truly unique. There is no one else like you in the universe, and you have hidden and unique talents to develop, explore, and share with the world.

Volumes have been written about dharma and discovering your dharma. Put most simply, you will know your dharma because it's the activity you find the most joy in doing. You lose track of time while doing it, it brings joy to you and others and somehow serves the greater good. It could be playing or writing music, or creating art, or curing illness. It could be woodworking or teaching or designing great works of architecture. Your dharma could be helping people with their finances, running a bakery, or being a master mechanic or a mindful groundskeeper. It could be any number of things, but part of your life's purpose is to discover what it is. Develop it, nurture it, and share it with others.

When your intentions are in line with your dharma, the world truly conspires to bring them to fruition.

Practice: Make a list of the things you love to do and talents you've always wanted to explore. If you're working at a job or in a profession that you don't feel is your dharma, and you find little joy in it but need to pay the bills, explore your passion in your free time. Instead of watching TV, playing video games, or wasting time in some other fruitless endeavor, develop your talent. Nurture it. Imagine living it and doing it every day. Then, when the time is right, you will be ready. Use meditation, faith, and the power of intention to make your dreams a reality.

That's what I've done with writing. I love God. I love to write and inspire others. I was inspired to write this for you. I didn't quit everything else I was doing at the time, but I woke up early in the morning, meditated, prayed, and wrote. It came to me easily, and I lost track of time while doing it. I believe it serves the greater good. I would wake up with what needed to be written already in my mind, and even if it were four in the morning, I would get up and write. You can do the same with your talents. Explore and develop them in your free time.

You are unique and made up of the stuff of stars
There is no one quite like you
Find what you're meant to give to the world
Discover your true calling

Live it
Love it
Share it

And in doing so
Feel your Oneness
With the underlying
Creative force of the Universe.

Loving Service

Faith in action is love, and love in action is service.
—MOTHER TERESA

WE WERE BORN TO SERVE OTHERS. YOU HAVE KNOWN IT from a young age. When you saw someone suffering, you wanted to help them. When you saw someone hungry, you wanted to feed them or give them all the money in your pocket. When you saw someone feeling sad, you wanted to comfort them. These are a child's natural tendencies. As we grow up, sometimes, the world can harden us, and we begin to forget our true nature.

I don't really watch much TV anymore, but I remember years ago, watching television, and a commercial would come on about poverty in Africa; orphans who needed food, clothing, and education, and my heart would ache, and the tears would stream down my face. I would end up adopting one of the kids in the commercial. They send you a picture in the mail and a description of what your donation is doing for them. This is our nature. Part of a human being's dharma is to help and serve.

Find a way to serve. When you feel joy inside, it can be as simple as sharing it with a smile. Just your beautiful smile can change and brighten someone's day. Find a way to serve in your work, outside of work, and in your relationships. One thing I often silently ask when meeting people is: *How can I serve you? How can I understand you?* The more I say the prayer of St. Francis, and the more I meditate and utilize my mantra, the more this has become my natural way of thinking. *How can I serve you?*

That's a good way to enter a conversation or interaction with family, friends, a customer, or someone in need.

How can I serve you?

It is in giving that we receive, it is in pardoning that we are pardoned, and it is in dying that we are born to eternal life.

—ST. FRANCIS OF ASSISI

The "dying" that St. Francis talks about here is the dying of the ego; the dying of that which separates us from God, and the God in all beings. When the ego is no more, we are reborn to eternal life *in* this life. We become peaceful, kind, generous, loving, and giving. We can become like St. Francis, Thich Nhat Hanh, Mother Teresa, and Gandhi through the death of the ego, selfless service, and living our life's purpose.

Practice: The next time you have an interaction with those close to you in life, silently ask the question: "How can I serve you?" and then find out. What do they need that you may have been missing or neglecting? It could be your spouse or children, a family member, a co-worker, or someone you have an interaction with at the grocery. Think of all the ways you serve now, and of all the ways you could serve that you may be missing out on. If you're a parent, include your children in some way. Teach them the joy of service: building a deck, participating in a food drive, serving in line at the homeless food kitchen. The possibilities are endless, and there is no better way to spend time with those you love than in service to others.

In your suffering and in your pain
In your tears that fall like rain

In your loneliness and despair
I see myself, That's why I'm here

Let me lend you my strength and give you my faith
My hope, my love and our mother's grace

Your grateful smile reveals her face
The Divine Mother of our human race

Bright like the sun, in a clear blue sky
She awakens our hearts and opens our eyes

To the truth of this world and to all of its lies
Her gift is a love that can't be denied

It's in loving and giving that we receive
In praying sincerely from down on our knees

In caring for those who are sorely in need
That our little raindrop returns to the sea.

ETERNITY

Possessions fade and turn to rust
Our house decays and turns to dust
This old body will pass away
Not to live another day

Buried deep inside the ground
Never again to be found
Or burned to ash by fires bright
My soul moves on into the light

Beyond the stream my spirit soars
To lighter realms and distant shores
Awakened from this cosmic dream
I understand what sages mean

Leave the shadows of the cave
Live the wisdom that they gave
Love and light that never fades
Eternity was never made

Underneath the weight of who you have been taught to believe you are lies the Divine Self, full of love and light, beyond duality and judgment, beyond pain and suffering. This is your true self and your true nature; the source from which manifests all love, creativity, and joy.

—OM, PEACE, AMEN—

Recommended Reading

When I look over at my bookshelf, out of the hundreds of books I have read and studied on spirituality and religion, these are the ones that stand out to me, the ones that gave me those "aha moments" we so yearn for in life. I have read many of them more than once and some a dozen times.

I considered ranking them but decided that valuing a book's content can be very subjective. How you feel about a book and what you are able to learn from it greatly depends on where you currently are along your spiritual journey. I remember picking up *The Autobiography of a Yogi* from my mother's bookshelf several times over a period of years before finally deciding to read it. When I finally did start it, I couldn't put it down, and have since read it many times. A similar thing happened with *The Power of Now*, and every time I read or listen to it, I learn something new. So, I settled for alphabetical order. You can decide how to rank the ones you've read or the ones that you decide to read.

Illusions, by Richard Bach

The Seven Spiritual Laws of Success, by Deepak Chopra

The Alchemist, by Paulo Coelho

The Hidden Gospel, by Neil Douglas-Klotz

The Bhagavad Gita, translated by Eknath Easwaran

The Upanishads, translated by Eknath Easwaran

The Tao Te Ching, by Lao Tzu; translated by Gia-Fu Feng
    and Jane English

Man's Search for Meaning, by Victor Frankl

The Way to God, by Mahatma Gandhi

The Prophet, by Kahlil Gibran

Being Peace, by Thich Nhat Hanh

Old Path White Clouds, by Thich Nhat Hanh

The Dhammapada, translated by Ananda Maitreya,
    foreword by Thich Nhat Hanh

The Torah, the Bible and Kriya Yoga, by Paramahansa
    Prajnanananda

The Yoga Sutras of Sage Patanjali, translation and
    commentary by Paramahansa Prajnanananda

Getting the Buddha Mind, by Chan Master Sheng-Yen

Subtle Wisdom, by Chan Master Sheng-Yen

The Sivananda Companion to Yoga, by The Sivananda
    Yoga Center

Zen Mind, Beginner's Mind, by Shunryu Suzuki

The Essene Gospel of Peace, by Edmond Bordeaux Szekely

The Power of Now, by Eckhart Tolle *I recommend the
    audible version*

The Yoga of Jesus, by Paramahansa Yogananda

The Autobiography of a Yogi, by Paramahansa Yogananda

The Holy Bible, *KJV and NIV **specifically "The Sermon on the Mount"

About the Author

OLIVER BARDWELL IS A WRITER, POET, ENTREPRENEUR, life coach, and author of *The Way: A Small Book of Wisdom*. He has been studying and practicing Kriya Yoga, meditation, and the Chinese martial arts for decades, and has spent a lifetime learning about religion and spirituality. Growing up with an amazing mother, who was not only a devout Christian but also a locally renowned and gifted psychic, Oliver learned to view life as a mystical journey. As we read his writing and poetry, this becomes apparent, and a world of magic and spirit begins to open up to us.

Connect with Oliver:

www.oliverbardwell.com

Made in the USA
Monee, IL
12 June 2021

70791282R00111